Ⓐ

A YEAR OR SO AGO, TIM CURRAN AND CHRISTIAN FLETCHER WERE BOTH CAPTIVATED BY THE SUPERMAN MOVE PERFORMED BY MOTOCROSS RIDERS. SOON, BOTH WERE REGULARLY MAKING THE MANEUVER. IMAGINE, YOU, UP HERE, LIKE TAJ, FLYING INTO THE SETTING SUN.

BOOK OF THE SURFING

IMAGINE
HOW GOOD
IT WOULD FEEL IF

YOU SURFED LIKE

TAJ BURROW...

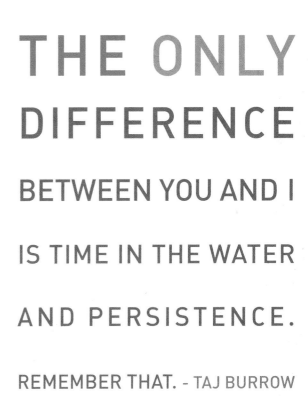

THE ONLY DIFFERENCE

BETWEEN YOU AND I

IS TIME IN THE WATER

AND PERSISTENCE.

REMEMBER THAT. - TAJ BURROW

EDITED BY SAM McINTOSH

PUBLISHED BY ROLLINGYOUTH PRESS. 2003

A

B

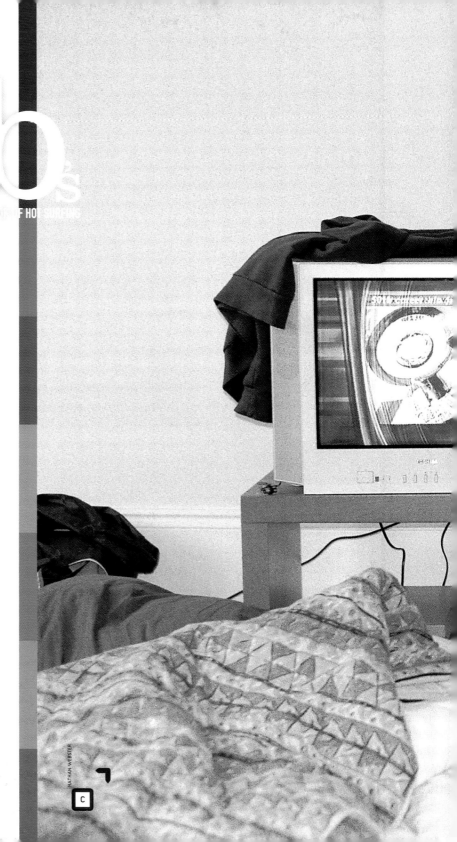

C

FROM TAJ

There is no way in hell I could survive away from the ocean. Being able to play in the ocean every day is essential for me. I can't function away from the coast. This year I spent some time in Switzerland, Las Vegas, Arizona and London. Even though I had such a good time at all those places I was physically and mentally freaked out being so far inland. It amazes me to think of people who have never seen the ocean and probably never will! It's so heavy that they don't know what they're missing. I wish I could somehow tell them. I love surfing! There is nothing cooler than riding unpredictable waves with your own style and approach. Faced with sections and thinking, floater? air? reverse? carve? or whatever the hell you want. No waves or conditions are ever the same. How could you ever get sick of it? Yeah, it's my job, but even if it wasn't I would do what I can to surf every day of my life. The only thing better than surfing is surfing well. And that's what this book's all about.

TAJ HAS TWO CRIBS, ONE IN YALLINGUP (B) AND ANOTHER IN LONDON (A AND C). SEE, WITH LONDON BEING SUCH A TRAVEL HUB, TO CUT HIS TIME IN THE AIR HE WILL SPEND A DAY OR TWO IN THE ENGLISH CAPITAL BETWEEN FLIGHTS. HE'S HAPPIEST, THOUGH, WHEN HE'S AT (B), STANDING ON HIS BALCONY AND FEELING A WARM EASTERLY OFFSHORE ON HIS BACK.

CONTENTS

WHERE YOU AT?

This is not a typical how-to book. It has no instant solutions. You may learn some things from it quickly, think you're doing okay, then one day everything will go wrong. You will pound your board with your fists because it keeps bogging a maneuver. You will miss waves, and swear like an obnoxious fool. And you will have sessions that are so disappointing you'll wanna jam your board into the car park bitumen until it's in pieces. Think it's easy, once you know how? Forget it. Stop reading now. Frustration and anger are regular companions to anyone who wants to surf well.

That's because a good surfer knows the rewards. When it comes together, your feet and arms and torso move in ways you didn't know were possible. Your board becomes not only a high-speed projectile, but crazily loose and responsive as well. And the ocean becomes the ultimate playground. This book will hopefully shortcut you to those magic days.

It's divided into four color-coded sections. How easily you pick up the moves depends on your level of skill. If you fail, repeat, repeat, repeat. You will get there eventually. On the way, you will be thinking about your surfing, thinking about your emotions, and realizing you can improve. Each page also has a TB Tip — little things I've picked up along the way, things you would have worked out for yourself eventually, but I'm passing on to you now.

And to complete the picture, I've got Derek Rielly, one of Australia's greatest ever surf-mag editors, to throw in some tips about keeping the flame burning when you're back on land. Learning to surf is gonna change your life. That's a cool thing. You'll want to change some of your priorities, and maybe get rid of some things that you don't need any more. It's all part of the life. Derek knows, because he's lived it and loved it for more than twenty years.

Alright. Now, let's go surfing.

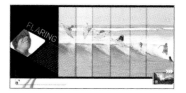

A. TB, THE GATEKEEPER, HOLDING THE ANSWERS FOR YOU IN ONE OF FOUR COLOR-CODED SECTIONS.

A

SWINGING IT 'ROUND OFF THE BOTTOM AT LANCE'S LEFTS IN INDONESIA. THE EYES DO ALL THE TALKING HERE.

EARLY DAYS

You can always learn to surf. You may not attack the tour or throw down alley oops but you can experience the rush of moving across a wave. I started at seven and I can't really remember life without surf. How quickly you pick it up is like all things in life. Some are down with maths, others football. I've seen guys take up surfing at the same time, surf together everyday and one will shine while the other gets it slowly. If you're under 12, you're in the glory days. If you're under 15, chances are you'll be a good surfer. World Championship Tour surfer, Lee Winkler didn't start surfing until he was 14. If you're starting late in your teens, you can still get an act though you'll have to work hard to get a good style. If you're starting in your twenties or later, you'll have to put in some real time but don't be too disheartened. The youth advantage is more environmental, I reckon. When you're young you have no kids, no job, no wife, no worries... just school, surf, surf vids in those glory years. Who in their twenties can spend every weekend surfing eight hours a day? The first four years are crucial. Improving'll be about your attitude, not your level of skill. Be keen, have fun, you'll improve without knowing...

globe

NAME	AGE	HEIGHT	WEIGHT	DIMENSIONS
Luke Egan	32	5'11"	198 lb	6'4" × 19" × 2 1/2"
Mark Occhilupo	37	5'9"	176 lb	6'3" × 18 3/4" × 2 3/8"
Andy Irons	25	6'0"	165 lb	6'2" × 18 1/4" × 2 1/4"
Joel Parkinson	22	5'11"	161 lb	6'2" × 18 1/4" × 2 1/4"
Shane Dorian	31	5'9"	155 lb	6'0" × 18 1/4" × 2 1/4"
Kalani Robb	25	5'9"	155 lb	6'0" × 18 1/4" × 2 1/8"
Taj Burrow	24	5'9"	150 lb	5'11" × 17 3/4" × 2 1/8"

A

A. IMAGINE, MASTER SHAPER GREG WEBBER PAYS YOU TO ACCEPT AND RIDE TWENTY-TWO NEW 5'11S! WHAT A LIFE MR BURROW LEADS! B. STINKING SUITS... OUT!

CHOOSING A BOARD

I HAVE ALL OF MY BOARDS CUSTOM MADE. AND FOR THE PAST FIVE YEARS, I'VE BEEN ORDERING THE SAME 5'11" × 17 3/4" × 2 1/8" BOARDS AS MY STANDARD SHORT BOARD. AFTER A FEW YEARS, YOU KNOW EXACTLY WHAT YOU WANT. UNTIL THEN, HERE'S WHAT TO LOOK FOR...

Don't order a custom board as your first surfboard. If everything goes well, you'll improve quickly and your boards will change accordingly. Boards are like cars: low resale value. Take a board out of the showroom, have one surf on it, and you'll struggle to get $200 for it on the second-hand racks.

Make your first board one of those spongey learners' jobs. You don't need high performance yet, just something that won't hurt you when you fall off. Round-nose boards are good too. They're safer and the extra volume up the nose makes the board more stable.

If you learn on a high-performance board, you will end up with an atrocious style. I swear. A big board is harder to turn and duckdive but it will make your technique so much better in the long run. Trust me, you'll draw smoother lines and be a better surfer – and sooner – for it.

When you're buying a second-hand board, look out for open dings. They'll take in water, making your board heavier and yellow. Don't worry too much about pressure dings, a slightly sunken deck or one that isn't gleaming white. These are not fatal faults, and you can use them to bring the price down. Keep an eye out for previous snaps, though. You should be able to see where they've fixed it. This is not fatal either, but make sure the board does not feel too heavy, and you get a fair deal. Anything over about $150 is a bit rich if it's been broken. Pull off stickers or rub them to make sure there are no open dings underneath.

Here's the advice from Rodney Dahlberg, Occy's shaper:

Beginner

A board has three functions: duck-diving, paddling and riding. A board that's too big for you will help you master all of these things. You'll develop a smooth surfing style, and when you eventually get on a shorter board, it will feel crazily responsive.

Getting better

So you've learnt to take off and trim. Here's a guide to the size of the board you should now be riding...

WEIGHT	DIMENSIONS
- 110 lb	5'9" × 17 ½" × 2"
111-125 lb	5'10" × 17 ¾" × 2 ⅛"
126-140 lb	6'0" × 18" × 2 ⅛"
141-155 lb	6'0" × 18 ¼" × 2 ³⁄₁₆"
156-170 lb	6'2" × 18 ⅜" × 2 ¼"
171-185 lb	6'3" × 18 ½" × 2 ⁵⁄₁₆"
186-200 lb	6'4"-6'6" × 18 ¾" × 2 ⅜"
Over 200 lb	Big stinking tank

These are based on standard builds. Your height affects length of the board; your weight affects the volume (width and thickness). The best place to buy a surfboard is from a shaper. If he's a nice guy (most of 'em are), he'll be keen to make you a board that works, rather than getting a quick buck. Surf shops are cool, as long as the staff know their stuff. Pawn shops can cough up good deals but you need to know exactly what you're looking for.

Being your best

As your surfing improves, your boards will get smaller. Your dimensions should morph into something between the pros' boards and those above. At the left are the dimensions of pros' boards. However, you will see similar-size boards ridden by completely different-size surfers. Why? Because the one crucial measurement that board makers don't provide is volume, which is determined by the curve of the rails.

TB TIP

THE INCUBATOR. I'm pretty useless with the little things in life but I make sure every time I get out of the car after a surf, I'll at least dump my wet wetties and towels on the porch. I never hang 'em up but I'll get em out of the car, otherwise next time you get in, your ride will have picked up the crookest stench ever.

CURVED FINS

MORE BITE
MORE HOLD
MORE RESPONSE
LESS PREDICTABLE

STRAIGHT FINS

SMOOTHER TRANSITIONS
THRU TURNS —
SIMPLE
CLEAN
MORE PREDICABLE

STANDARD FOIL
SAFE SIMPLE - WORKS WELL

HIGH LIFT FOIL -
PULLS QUICKLY INTO THE FACE
VERY RESPONSIVE - NEW DIRECTION

SAFE
FAT DULL RAIL
^

MORE CRITICAL
RESPONSIVE FINE RAIL
^

MODERN MIX OF THE 2.

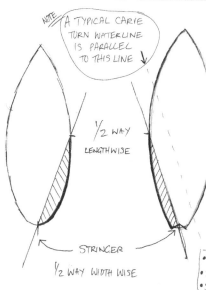

NOTE → A TYPICAL CARVE TURN WATERLINE IS PARALLEL TO THIS LINE ↓

½ WAY LENGTHWISE

STRINGER

½ WAY WIDTH WISE

IF YOU DRAW AN
IMAGINARY LINE THRU
THESE POINTS,
THE CHUNK OF RAIL
HIGHLIGHTED, GIVES
THE MOST CHARACTER
TO YOUR TURNS.
• GREATER CURVE GIVE
• GREATER RESPONSE.
LESS CURVE GIVES MORE
HOLD AND DRIVE.

• CURVY ROUND TAIL IS PIVOTAL
• STRAIGHT SWALLOW IS DRIVEY
• SQUARE TAIL IS A GOOD BLEND

MORE BITE + SPEED
CONCAVE

LIVELY AND PREDICTABLE
FLAT

DULL, BUT GREAT WITH WIDTH
VEE

NOTE — SLIGHTLY CURVED FINS
WITH MODERATE RAKE AND
WITH LIFTING FOILS
⟹ THE NEXT THING

DRIVE
HOLD
DIRECTION
STIFFNESS

BASE
WIDTH

RESPONSE
SLICE
DRIFT
LOOSENESS

A. FEEL THE THICKNESS, SIGHT THE CURVE, SCOPE THE OUTLINE. STILL, EVEN THE SHARPEST EYE CANNOT TELL FOR SURE IF A BOARD WILL WORK. ONLY THING TO DO IS... TRY IT! HAND-DRAWN DIAGRAMS BY GREG WEBBER. B. CLEAN BOARDS, CLEAN MIND.

NAVIGATING YOUR BOARD

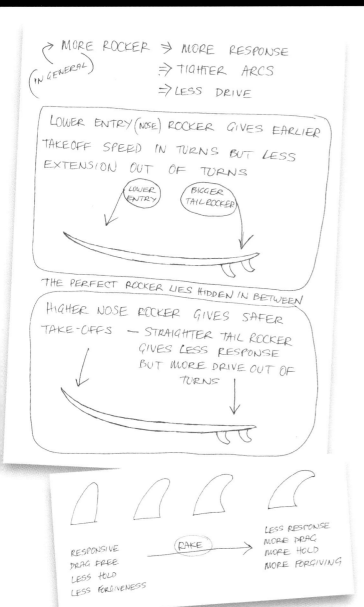

> MORE ROCKER ⇒ MORE RESPONSE
(IN GENERAL) ⇒ TIGHTER ARCS
⇒ LESS DRIVE

LOWER ENTRY (NOSE) ROCKER GIVES EARLIER TAKEOFF SPEED IN TURNS BUT LESS EXTENSION OUT OF TURNS

LOWER ENTRY   BIGGER TAIL ROCKER

THE PERFECT ROCKER LIES HIDDEN IN BETWEEN

HIGHER NOSE ROCKER GIVES SAFER TAKE-OFFS — STRAIGHTER TAIL ROCKER GIVES LESS RESPONSE BUT MORE DRIVE OUT OF TURNS

RESPONSIVE
DRAG FREE
LESS HOLD
LESS FORGIVENESS

RAKE ⟶

LESS RESPONSE
MORE DRAG
MORE HOLD
MORE FORGIVING

BECAUSE BOARDS ARE SO TECH AND CONFUSING AND SHAPERS LOVE TALKING ABOUT THE CRAFT, I'VE HANDED THIS PAGE OVER TO MY SHAPER, GREG WEBBER.

TB is really easy to work with. He asks for changes in terms of length, width and thickness when he thinks he needs to go up a touch. He's getting more powerful every few months so I need to deliver more hold so he can't over-power his craft. Whether the next change is bigger fins or less rocker and planshape curve in the tail, who knows? We'll try a few things.

I made Taj 20 short boards in one go last year and that really helped him mentally. He didn't have to worry about where I was in the world or whether his next batch would arrive in time. It also meant that 90 per cent of them were fully cured by the time he got to try them, which is almost never with most top pros.

One thing he has changed is his openness to experiment. Once he has a good batch of boards, like three back-ups for his normal board, I'll give him some fins-forward designs, which we have been working on. Taj has also been experimenting with fin foils so he's reached a good balance of having the reliable contest quiver and the mini experimental quiver.

Overall, I prefer going out to the special clubs with Taj and Stamos and not mentioning one thing about boards. I remember giving him some new boards at Huntington after the contest there. We spent 15 seconds looking at the sticks before he said we should go for a walk through the flesh gallery outside. Crazy G-stringed women with bum tattoos were arcing their asses at us. I'm glad he and I share a similar responsiveness toward

sexy females.

Of course, all guys love sexy chicks, but we are generally hopeless at tuning. Taj is no wanker, he's just confident with women. I've watched two performers compete for him at a special club in the hope that they might catch him as a ticket out of that field of expression.

He can be hard on them too. He showed me a text message. I said: "Well, that's the end of her, huh!" He replied: "You'd be amazed what I can get away with, she'll write back and just pretend that I was joking." A minute later, he smirks and reads me her expected response. Ah, feminists would love him. Me too, for that matter.

TB TIP

LIL DINGS. Wax in a ding isn't water tight. Tape or stickers don't actually work because water always gets in there. I get little blowouts everywhere then check out my board and see all these rancid brown rings and am so rattled. It's easy to keep a board in good condition. Fix 'em quick and you'll be fine.

globe

A. KEEP THE BLOCK AT ANGLE AND SWIPE GREAT SWATHES OF GRIPPING WAX ACROSS THE DECK. B. QUICK HUMPS, THE CLOSEST THING TO GOLD YOU'LL FIND FOR AROUND A BUCK. C. PADDLE HARD, REAP THE WHIRLWIND.

WAXING UP

[AND GETTING PERFECT HUMPS] PG // 019

I'M REALLY BAD AT CHANGING WAX. I LIKE KEEPING THE THICKEST, UGLIEST WAX JOB ON THERE. I DON'T LIKE THE LOOK OF IT BUT I JUST LOVE HOW IT FEELS. PLUS, TAKING THE WAX OFF IS THE WORST CHORE IN THE WORLD.

What's weird on the tour is the rules other people have. Shane Powell takes his wax off before every heat. He goes out with these real thin wax jobs. I don't know how he doesn't slip off every wave. He's gnarly.

WAX ON, WAX OFF...

▶ A few things give you dirty wax. Wetsuits are a killer. No matter what colour wetsuit you wear, you're gonna give your wax some dodgy pigmentation. You might not win the battle to stop your board going yellow in the sun, but at least you can keep your wax clean.

▶ Wanna keep it clean? Don't surf with dirty feet from tar on the road. Rub your feet in the sand or on the rocks before you get out there. And don't let your wax melt in the sun in the car. Somehow the gear ends up dirty and brown.

▶ It's all about personal preference. Some people go by the two-week rule. If they're riding the same board every day, they change their wax every two weeks. The good thing about having a nice thick coating of wax is that if you don't wax up every session, you can still make it it sticky with a wax comb.

▶ Where? I tend to cover most of my board with wax, from in front of my tailpad almost to the nose. Even though I rarely put my feet right on the front, it's crucial for emergencies. I've been making airs and seeing them on video and my foot's right on the beak. Also, I shimmy up the deck in the tube. You might have seen people with a wax patch just big enough for their feet. In a word? Gibbons. If you try to surf on that, you have either the most boring

surfing technique on earth or spend a lot of time falling off. A frontside air or a backside reo with your feet in the same place? Yeah right...

▶ Application. It's best to apply wax to a perfectly clean board. A wax comb will get the bulk of the gear off and a cloth and elbow grease will get the rest. For a slick look, use acetone. Or grab some foam dust from your local shaper's den. Rub a handful of the stuff over the wax and she'll come straight off. It makes a mess, though, so don't do it inside or your folks will turn.

▶ Sweet bumps. You might have seen your dad or some of the older crew throw down their block of wax flat and circle to blind victory. I say blind, because flat waxing is going against the grain to perfect bumps. The deal? Put your wax on edge when you wax up, say at a 45-degree angle and make diagonal stripes criss-crossing down your board with a corner of the block. After this, keep your wax at an angle with a flat section rubbing over where the bumps are. Keep rubbing it on evenly over the entire waxed surface. I assure you, lumps will appear.

▶ If you want to get really pedantic, you can use a cold-water-wax base, then a warm-water-wax coat on top. I use Sex Wax (Quick Humps). Red label for base, orange for the coat. Get this process round the wrong way and you'll just rub off the base, and be left with an almost unridable board. It's weird, I know.

What isn't cool is sand in your wax. It makes it slippery and impossible to put more wax on. Wet sand is okay

for roughing up your wax. Dry sand is a no-no. Don't lay your board deck-down on the sand on a hot day.

▶ Combs roughen your wax when it's slippery, which is handy when you haven't got any wax. If you're running a tight ship as far as clean, consistent waxing goes (yes, it is an art!), avoid the comb. They work best when you're sporting really thick gear.

▶ When using a wax comb, scratch diagonally from rail to rail using the side with the teeth on it. If you're stuck, use your fingernails or a seashell.

TB TIP

PADDLE HARD FOR WAVES. People do it all the time, especially in Hawaii. It helps you get waves in a crowd. The first one who twitches, the first one who bolts, who paddles and kicks and splashes and looks down the line, usually gets the wave. They're committed. If I've got the inside and someone's kicking and splashing and looking like they really want it and are looking down the line, I'm just like "Aaah, fricken go then..."

A. TAJ AND HIS OLD BOY VANCE AT J-BAY. VANCE, A CLASSIC EX-PAT AMERICAN WHO WAILS ON GUITAR, HAS BEEN TAKING HIS BOY UP TO THE BLUFF AND GNARALOO EVEN BEFORE THE KID COULD SURF, AND BEGAN FILMING HIM ON VIDEO WELL BEFORE TAJ BECAME A BLIP ON THE SURF MAG RADAR. EVEN HIS MOM NANCY SURFS! WHAT A FAMILY! B. SEND THE ENTRIES, KIDS, PRIZES ARE WAITING TO BE COLLECTED.

HOW TO

MAKE THE MOST OF YOUR YOUTH [WORDS BY DEREK RIELLY]

GET YOUR ACT TOGETHER NOW AND YOU WILL RULE ALL THROUGH YOUR LIFE...

A smart cat once said, "Youth is wasted on the young". How true it is! You eat crap, f**k anything that walks, crawls or slithers, drink like a maniac and drive fast and careless. From teenagehood to your mid-twenties you will believe you are immortal. You will drive drunk, pick fights with the wrong people, and perform handstands on high-rise balconies. Most of you will survive. Some won't.

But the one thing you've gotta remember amid all these good times is that one day you will be thirty-five, forty, fifty, sixty even. And the groundwork you lay down now will prepare your body and mind for the ageing process. It's ain't too cool getting old, but do the right thing now and it won't be so rough.

1. Eat good. Lay off the fried, greasy gear. Maccas and KFC actually taste better in moderation. Stuff like oatbran and bananas for breakfast, salad sandwich for lunch and then fish or pasta for dinner will feed and please your body.

2. Wear condoms. It ain't about AIDS or radical diseases that wreck your womb scraper, it's about babies, kids. One unprotected spasm inside a fertile hole and you could be paying maintenance for the next 18 years as well has having the responsibility of a helpless human being on your shoulders.

3. Work out a way to make money. There's too many cats out there, thirty-plus, who smoked weed and drank beer all through their twenties thinking they were somehow beating the system and who are now stuck working long hours in factories to support a family. Not all of us can be pro surfers but there are plenty of other cool gigs out there.

4. Stretch. Who wants to be a bent old man that can't get out of bed?

5. Be kind to good friends. Remember birthdays and talk 'em up when they're not around. Always choose quality over quantity. Cool crowds don't last forever. Remember those mates who you hung with before you were swept up with the groovies.

6. Chill in the car and leave the tire-burning gear to the kids who don't surf. They've got nothing to live for. You've got a lifetime of waves.

7. Always buy the best you can afford whether it's food, coffee beans or a surfboard. Life's too short to eat, ride, f**k or drink crap.

TB TIP

YOU'VE GOTTA BE IN IT... TO... WIN IT! Seriously, enter competitions in magazines. You know how you flick past them because, like, you'll never win? Most mags receive way less entries than you'd expect. Whack something together, be a little creative (color in the envelope if you have to) and bang it in the post. Likewise, if you're ever writing something, write how you speak. There're no rules. Let your own personality shine.

A. TAJ, WORLD CHAMP ANDY IRONS AND JOEL PARKINSON CHECK OUT THE GLASSY CONDITIONS AT BACKDOOR PIPE ON OAHU'S NORTH SHORE. WHAT LOOKS LIKE AN EASY RIDE IS A SLAUGHTERHOUSE OVER HARD, SHALLOW ROCK. ALL THREE ARE SMART ENOUGH TO ASSESS THE JOINT BEFORE PADDLING OUT. B. AND WHAT BETTER PLACE TO SIT UP ON YOUR BOARD AND TAKE IN THE VIEW: SUMATRA'S MACARONIS.

THE RIGHT CONDITIONS

YOU'LL LEARN THE FILTER PRETTY QUICKLY. WHAT IS THE FILTER? WELL, IT'S NOT AN ACCEPTED TERM — YET — BUT IT'S WHAT I APPLY TO OTHER PEOPLE'S SURF REPORTS. SEE, IN AMERICA, A HEAD-HIGH WAVE IS SIX FEET. BUT CALL SIX FEET ON A HEAD-HIGH WAVE IN HAWAII AND EVERYONE THINKS YOU'RE SOFT.

"Brah, you tink that wave was six foot eh? Maybe three feet... max!" You'll hear this conversation many times on the North Shore, I swear. It's hilarious. You will eventually learn to apply the filter to the various reports you hear: on the radio, the internet, the news, and from your mates. Wave size is arbitrary. You'll work it out.

REALITY CHECK...

▶ It feels good to rock up to a beach where there's waves and leap straight into it. But if you're a beginner, don't. Study the conditions first. Not only will you avoid getting into trouble, you'll catch more waves.

▶ Check for rips. If you see a section of brown, sandy water at a beachbreak, it's probably a rip (the channel that sends all the water from incoming waves back out to sea). You might see one that's only flowing gently, or not even flowing at all, and think, pah! But wait till after a set. Bang! Suddenly it's the raging Nile. Here's the tip: don't worry. At most, it's only gonna take you out 100 yards or so. But if you wanna get out of its evil clutches before then, easy, just paddle sideways. As your surfing gets better, you will learn to love rips. I freak out on them. It's hard to stay in the take-off zone but once you get a wave, it's music! You get crazy, steep faces with smashable sections. And when you're done you can lay on your board and get a free ride back to the take-off zone.

▶ Check for currents. Watch the surfers already out there. Are they constantly paddling? Are they having trouble staying in, or even getting to, the take-off zone? If so, you'd better be up for a tough session. How long can you paddle non-stop for? One hour? Two? What will happen if you get tired, and the current takes you down the beach, where there are rips and the sets are closing out? Usually the current is caused by the waves themselves (tide affects it too, especially near a rivermouth). If you're in one and start to get tired, paddle way wide of the break. I'm talking 200 yards. Out there, you can rest without losing headway, then burn back into the lineup with renewed energy to get a wave in. Don't just use up all your energy. Manage it, and think about it.

▶ Watch where other people paddle out. If they get licked, reassess. If they get out okay, follow 'em.

▶ Try to only surf breaks where there are surfers of similar ability to you. This way, you know you're not taking unknown risks. And don't go out if it's crowded. Wait a while. Crowd sizes vary a lot during the day.

▶ Know where the reef and rocks are. Line them up with landmarks before you paddle out. In severe situations, they only surprise you once.

▶ Don't be put off by onshore winds. A mild onshore gives you crazy sections to punt, waft and tear your filthy lines all over. All to yourself, too.

▶ When it's offshore, hunt the tube. You can get barrels in onshore surf too but offshore waves are gold for barrels.

▶ Know the tides. If someone asks, "When's high?" you'll impress the hell out of them if you know. Knowing the tide can also help you decide whether conditions will improve or go to seed. If you've got a shorebreak closing out and fat waves out the back running into a gutter, chances are that on high tide the waves will stop breaking out the back and the shorey will be fun. Likewise, if there's a peak and it's still a bit fat, you could be in for some fast runners with a bit less tide.

TB TIP

SIT UP AND SHUT DOWN. Rather than have to paddle around for the entire session with your neck and head propped up off your board, you'll notice other surfers sitting in the line-up. It's tricky at the start but grab both rails about two-thirds of the way up your board. Pull yourself forward while at the same time pulling your board under yourself so you're sitting up. Take your hands off the rails and use your legs to keep you upright. This extra height also makes it easier for you to see what's coming.

A

A. TB'S BEST FRIEND DAMON 'STAMOS' NICHOLLS, PERFECTLY PLACED TO TAKE OFF ON THIS WESTERN AUSTRALIAN REBOUND. B. RIDE A BIGGER BOARD AND YOU'VE GOT THE STANDING PISTONS FIRED WELL BEFORE THE WAVE STANDS UP. C. "YEAH MATE, I'M BROKEN DOWN ON A DIRT TRACK, I'LL BE THERE SOON."

PADDLING

AT ONE POINT IN YOUR SURFING LIFE, YOU'LL BE PADDLING, UTTERLY EXHAUSTED AND THE SURF WILL BE TOO GOOD TO GO IN. YOUR ARMS WILL THROB WITH PAIN AS IF EVERY BIT OF ENERGY HAS BEEN ZAPPED FROM THEM. THING IS, YOU'LL KEEP PADDLING BECAUSE GOOD SURF IS BETTER THAN ANYTHING ON EARTH. THAT NIGHT, THERE'LL BE NO BETTER FEELING THAN THE SATISFACTION OF WHAT YOU'VE DONE. YOU WAIT.

Some people get paddling, others don't. They'll have well-built rigs and a wave'll approach them and they just can't catch it. Others will be way outside of where waves are breaking and yet somehow they'll still coast into waves. Seems weird, but it isn't. It's all about technique.

PADDLE POWER...

▶ Paddling is made a lot easier if you practice in flat water. Before you take on the relentlessness of the ocean, try a swimming pool, lake or a really flat day. Time spent here will give you confidence and strength in the ocean.

▶ When lying on your board, the nose should be a few inches out of the water. Too much nose and you're wasting your paddle power. Too little and you're too far up the board. Or the board's too small for you.

▶ Always lay on the center of your board, with the stringer running down the center of your chest and in between your legs.

▶ Paddling with your legs apart and hanging over your rails looks crook and creates drag. At the start, your knees may hurt if they're together. They'll toughen quickly as will your shoulders and ribs. The pain will go away and remember, paddling's good for the rig.

▶ Depending on the size of the board you choose to ride, you should almost always have board under your shins and a lot of board above and beyond your face.

▶ Lift your chest, neck and head away from the deck of the board when you're paddling.

You need to see where you're going.

▶ Make nice, even, alternating strokes. Reach out beside the nose of your board, drive through the water and have your arm exit the water next to your legs. Steer clear of the double paddle. It's exhausting and not as effective. You may have seen surf lifesavers paddling on their knees. Leave it to 'em.

▶ The horn of your leash should be pointed to the outside of your ankle. If you can feel it, there's a good chance you'll trip on it when you catch a wave.

▶ To turn or change direction, just lean slightly to the side you want to go as if in a boat. Always hit waves front on, don't be sideways as a wave approaches.

▶ Sometimes waves look like they won't break but sometimes — mostly when it's onshore — waves will give you a little push. When you really want to move but you can't quite get on a wave, paddle with a faster stroke rate, move up your board a touch and place your chin close to the board. This will give you a lower center of gravity and helps transfer your paddle power into speed.

▶ Does kicking help? Mentally I'd say it would but I think your arms do all the work. You feel like you're more committed and it lifts your confidence so it's a good thing.

▶ If there's an approaching peak down the beach, you'd be surprised how much ground a good paddler can cover. You may not get it but if you do you're slowly becoming more of a waterman. You've read the ocean and moved accordingly.

Pointbreaks and crazy sweeps.

▶ If you're surfing somewhere like Kirra or that amazing bank at Snapper on the Gold Coast, you have to paddle all session just to hold your spot in the line-up. Swing wide, say 100 to 150 yards, and paddle around the main break. The sweep isn't so strong out wide and you'll overtake everyone else, who's close to the break. It's like swimming against a rip, there's always another option. The smart kids will be onto it.

TB TIP

THE ULTIMATE CRIME. Making a call you're gonna meet a mate at a beach, pick them up for a surf or saying you're gonna wait for a mate is inexcusable if you don't follow through. The ultimate sin. If you commit, stick to your word. Ignoring knocks on the door or turning your mobile off is seriously heavy. You're a mate, mate. Don't do it. Sure, it's grief when you've organized too big of a posse and you can't connect with everyone. Keep it small, keep it clean.

globe

02

04

A

A. PICTURE YOURSELF STROKING INTO A BOMB AT PIPE – THE LIP IS PITCHING, THE WATER IS RUSHING UP THE FACE, YOU PUSH YOURSELF UP AND... HOT CRAP... YOU'RE READY TO RIP. B. OKAY, YOU'RE NOT GOING TO FEEL REAL COOL BUT DOING A BIT OF BEACH WORK WILL FAST-TRACK THAT CLEAN STAND-UP MOTION. C. SUNSETS ARE EVEN MORE AWESOME FROM THE WATER.

PRACTICING ON THE BEACH

YOU'VE BOUGHT THE EQUIPMENT, YOU'VE CHECKED THE CONDITIONS, NOW IT'S TIME TO GET SOME OF THAT FREE LOVE FROM THE OCEAN. BUT BEFORE YOU GO DIPPING YOUR TOES, SLOW IT ON DOWN A SEC...

You're not going to get tubed this session. You're not going to bust an air. But you will, if you try hard enough, stand up. You are moments away from something very special. But, before you get out there, you must practice getting to your feet. The transition from lying to standing on your board is your first obstacle. Practice doing it on the beach first (push your fins into the sand so they don't crack or break). Rattled about practicing on the beach where people can see you? Don't be. This is the fastest, safest way to learn. Other surfers will respect you for it.

▶ Lay on your board with your feet hanging over the tail. Bring your hands up near your shoulders, and lightly lay them on the deck just inside the rails. You're going to place most of your weight between the bottom knuckle of your index finger and the inside heel of your palm. Now, quickly do a push-up, bringing your front foot under your chest to take most of your weight as you start to stand. Drag your back foot over the tail in a smooth motion and put it down about a third of the way up the board. Your front foot should be just past the middle. Both feet should be across the stringer. Do this 10 times.

UM, WHICH ONE IS MY FRONT FOOT?

▶ If you've ever snowboarded or skateboarded, you will know whether you're goofy or natural. A goofy has the right foot forward, a natural has the left foot forward. There is no known advantage or disadvantage of surfing either way. Neither is there likely to be one stance that suits you better. You are about to learn a combination of skills in which each leg, foot, arm and hand performs a unique function. As soon as you have chosen a stance – goofy or natural – the long learning process for each limb begins.

▶ Walk into the surf until the water's waist-to-chest high. This is where you'll be catching your first wave. You're just starting, remember, so don't go too deep. You're looking for a broken wave. When a wave is about 20 feet away, point the nose of your board to the beach and paddle hard. Don't let the wave hit you sideways.

▶ Hopefully the wave will pick you up and push you along. If it passes you by, you didn't paddle hard enough or you were lying too far back on the board. If your board dived and slid from under you, you were too far forward. If neither of these happens, though, and you find yourself being propelled by the wave, grab the rails and chill. Don't stand up yet. Enjoy the rush. Lean on each rail and feel how it makes the board turn. Do this a few times till you're ready for the next step.

▶ Now, all you have to do is exactly what you did on the sand. Jump up. Keep your feet across the stringer and concentrate on staying on for as long as you can. This is where you will thank me for advising you to buy a board that's not too short.

▶ When you get to your feet, keep your knees bent. Point your front arm to the beach, back arm to the wave. If you fall, it's usually because you're leaning too far in one direction. Don't

worry. Eventually you'll find the center of the board, and stand on it with confidence, if not style.

Now, let me get a little poetic here. When you finally get it right, resist the urge to paddle straight back out for another one. Instead, take a moment to etch every second of your first ride in your mind. Why? Because this, my friend, is the moment when your life changes forever. You've just tasted the magic of riding waves! No matter how good you get (and, with persistence, you will get good, very good), this stumbling, clumsy ride will remain a cherished memory as long as you live. Don't let it fade.

TB TIP

LEFT, LEFT, RIGHT, LEFT. When you're looking from the beach a lefthander breaks from left to right. A righthander breaks from right to left. Goofyfooters ride frontside on lefts, vice versa for regularfooters.

A

B

01

02

03

04

SEQUENCE: RESPONDEK.

A. THIS IS WHERE IT ALL BEGINS, A MADNESS THAT WILL TAKE OVER YOUR LIFE. B. GOING BACKSIDE, NOT ALMOST AS THREATENING AS YOU'D THINK. C. A LOW PROFILE, NOT A CREEPY DUNE SPRUIKER.

STANDING UP

[YOUR FIRST GREEN WAVE]

MY FIRST GREEN FACES WERE AT YALLINGUP WHEN I WAS ABOUT SEVEN. JUSTIN AND MELANIE REDMAN AND I WERE SURFING THE WHITEWATER, AND WE ALL DECIDED TO PADDLE OUT TO THE BACK OF THE REEF.

It was like the biggest thing in our lives. We caught a few, and were frothing over them. It was the best thing that had ever happened to us. A peak we'd never reach again. It seems so crazy to me now. Not that the excitement of that first time out the back ever really leaves you.

So this is where you're at now. You've dealt with standing up in the whitewater. Now you're ready to take your first drop. Find yourself a beachbreak where the waves are no bigger than waist high. Done that? Good.

LET THE MADNESS BEGIN...

▶ A green wave is an unbroken wave, a wave with a face. The water may be fluro blue or dark brown in color, but the unbroken wave is called the green face. Weird, I know, but hey, I didn't make the rules.

▶ When you stood up in the whitewater, you could do it in your own sweet time. Now, though, you'll be doing it at a critical moment. You must do it quickly and cleanly to get on the wave properly. Remember your foot placement: across the stringer, front foot near the middle, back foot just forward of the two side fins. As a beginner, the wider your stance, the more stable you'll feel. It looks pretty kooky, though. Eventually you will find the sweet spot instinctively, then you'll start making tiny adjustments for different waves and maneuvers. In the meantime, mark the spot in your wax if you want a guide.

▶ When you see a wave you want, and nobody's on your inside (see page 62), start making your move. When it's about 10 yards away, turn and paddle toward the beach, looking at the wave over your shoulder occasionally. You want the wave to come up behind you just as the lip is starting to pitch. Too early and you won't catch it. Too late and it'll break on top of you. Don't worry if your timing's out at first. You'll get it right after just a couple of waves.

▶ Before you stand up, be confident that what you're doing is not very extreme. The chance of you being hurt is really very slim. Water up your nose and sand in your tweeds is not pain.

▶ When the wave starts to pick you up, paddle a couple of extra-hard strokes, then jump to your feet. Don't coast down the face lying down, thinking you can stand up when you get to the bottom. You won't. You'll nosedive. Look at the bottom of the wave, and don't be frightened by the water rushing up toward you. Also, check where you're heading. If there's a surfer in your path who can't get out of your way, don't go.

▶ If the wave passes you by, you need more weight on your front foot and maybe move it a bit further forward. If that doesn't work, you're standing up too early, and probably not paddling hard enough.

▶ If you caught it properly, you will be one seriously happy surfer. How's the rush, eh? As long as you surf, the feeling you get when the wave picks you up, which is scary at first, never loses its thrill. Taking off is one of the basic joys of surfing.

▶ The first few times you ride a green face, forget about riding left or right. Just go straight. When you feel like turning, lean over your toes. This is your frontside direction (right if you're natural, left if you're goofy), which is easiest because it doesn't involve twisting your head. Basic turning in the wash shouldn't be too hard. If you've got this far, you're styling. Practise holding your front arm out and pointing it. See how your board follows? Cool, huh?

▶ By now you will be noticing that waves that don't close out, peel off left or right. To follow and travel with the green face, turn your head and arms the way the wave is breaking. This will send your board and body in that direction. Look down the line. Don't worry about how you look. You're on your feet. You're surfing!

▶ For most beginners, backside is riddled with mental anguish. But it's easy. The key? Centre your weight lower, and focus a little more on your heels and back foot. Again, watch the wave and point your front arm where you wanna go. At first, a wider stance will help.

▶ In the early days, you'll get sore ribs, rash on your chest, arms and thighs, weary shoulders, an aching back, and stiff leg muscles. Don't worry. You will not only get used to these various aches and pains, you'll learn to love them. I'm not a member of the "no pain, no gain" brigade, but these physical reactions are your body's way of telling you you pushed yourself to the limit today. It's so satisfying. Stay healthy (by surfing more) and you will always bounce back.

▶ Finally, get yourself a learning partner. Learning with a friend is easier because you can each see what the other's doing wrong, and talk about it. At the same time, you will be laying the foundation for a strong friendship. Dunno why it is, but people who surf together form really strong bonds. I guess, despite the occasional aggro, we're very lucky people. And we know it.

TB TIP

UNDERCOVER. If you're surfing a secret spot or somewhere which is fairly localized, keep it low key. Keep the stereo down in the carpark, don't walk out to the line-up in a pack of four (on your own's best, otherwise two) and let locals get their waves before you mount your wave assault. Localism and violent localism exist. Wear the blackest, mellowest wettie you own and play it cool. Catch the waves they don't want and don't yell to your mate across the lineup about how much you flared last wave.

A

A. WANT TO BE EQUIPPED TO GET OUT TO LINEUPS ALL OVER THE WORLD? ALL IT TAKES IS A SUBMERGED NOSE AND A WELL-PLACED KNEE OR FOOT. B. AND DON'T BE AFRAID OF FINE-TUNING YOUR ACT IN STILL WATER. C. SHOOTING HIS MOUTH OFF AT GNARALOO STATION TO HIS MATES BACK HOME. THE ADVANTAGE HERE? HIS MATES ARE A 12 HOURS DRIVE AWAY...

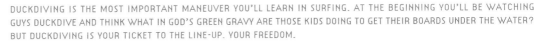

DUCKDIVING

(AND DEALING WITH ROLLING FOAM) PG // 031

DUCKDIVING IS THE MOST IMPORTANT MANEUVER YOU'LL LEARN IN SURFING. AT THE BEGINNING YOU'LL BE WATCHING GUYS DUCKDIVE AND THINK WHAT IN GOD'S GREEN GRAVY ARE THOSE KIDS DOING TO GET THEIR BOARDS UNDER THE WATER? BUT DUCKDIVING IS YOUR TICKET TO THE LINE-UP. YOUR FREEDOM.

It means you won't have to time lulls or only surf pointbreaks for the rest of your life. It means more waves and the more waves you catch, the more you improve. When you're first starting out, duckdiving is a major catch-22. See, you want to stand up as quickly as possible, so you buy a big, steady board. Thing is, you can't get that thing under the water to duckdive. Here's some techniques that will sort you out.

▶ What is a duckdive? It's the motion of paddling toward a broken wave or a wave about to break, sinking your board and body when the wave approaches, letting it pass over you and coming out unscathed on the other side. Well, in a perfect world anyway.

▶ The best way to duckdive a wave is to paddle hard toward it. This will give you momentum to penetrate. When it's almost on you, grip your rails and do a push-up, just as you practiced when you were learning to stand up (page 27), except this time you're trying to push your board into the water.

▶ Your legs play a massive role in the duckdive. If the oncoming wave isn't too heavy, just do a shallow duckdive by pushing one knee into the deck and straightening the other leg out. Try not to press too hard with your knee because you'll dent your board.

▶ For deep, critical duckdives, use your foot, like I do in the sequence here. Arch your foot forward, put your toes on the tail and push it down once you've got the nose as deep as it will go. The idea is for your board to be level when the wave passes over you.

▶ When you duckdive bigger waves, resist the urge to let go of your board. Your instinct will tell you it's unsafe to be tossed about underwater with it near you, but the truth is that you're safer hanging on. When the turbulence subsides, that board is going to shoot you to the surface. Without it, you're sinking. Even if you think you're upside down, don't panic. Gravity will sort things out real quick. After a few heavy duckdives your shoulders and arms will get stronger, and you'll learn to maneuver through the turbulence, back to the surface and the sweet air. You'll also be still on your board, ready to paddle for the wave behind while the gibbons who bailed are still frothing about in the impact zone.

▶ Sometimes the wave will be too big for your duckdiving skills, and you'll wanna jump off and swim deep instead. Cool. But look behind you first. If the wave has snuck up on you, there's a chance it has also snuck up on those around you. If someone is caught behind you, you must hang on. Let go of your board and it's going to hit him. You might even get entangled in each other's leashes. Bailing when someone is behind you is dangerous. Never, ever do it. Hang on, and the guy behind will respect you for it.

▶ When you're learning to duckdive, approach the wave straight on. You'll see other surfers paddling sideways and duckdiving, but don't do it yourself until you've got the hang of it.

▶ A clean duckdive through an unbroken wave can be an awesome experience, especially if the wave is really sucky. Look up just before you penetrate and watch the lip throw out across the sky – it's beautiful.

▶ And finally, the eternal question. Should you open your eyes down there? This is a weird one. People have told me that looking around underwater chills you out. Maybe, maybe not. But if you're at a sandy beachbreak. Keep 'em closed. That sand hurts! I only open them when it's heavy, like in Hawaii or Tahiti. It's so much easier when the water's clean, clear and warm.

TB TIP

KEEP IT CLOSED. If you've had a good surf and know of a sick little bank, you have to keep your mouth closed about it. It happens to me at home, I get all excited and tell a few people about an early I had. By the time it's lunch, word's out and you go back and everyone's all over it. It's tough but word of a fun bank spreads like a disease. Zip it, okay?

C

B

A. TB: OLDER, WISER AND A FREE-LIVING, FREE-LOVING, FIN-THROWING SOUL ON A RECENT TRIP TO THE MENTAWAIS. B. WHITE BOARDIES? RATTLED? AH, FAIR BITS...

COOL STORY

CODE RED PG // 033

A BUNCH OF MAD PRO SURFERS, INCLUDING TOM CARROLL, TURN THE BOY TAJ INTO A MAN DURING A WILD TRIP TO THE MENTAWAI ISLANDS, INDONESIA.HERE ARE SOME OF TAJ'S AND TOM'S MEMORIES OF THE TRIP...

Taj: This was my first major trip with a bunch of pros. I was 16. The Mentawais were virtually unknown back then, and there weren't many boats doing charters. I was riding for Quiksilver, and wanted to go on a trip more than anything. When they started organising it, I was the most excited kid in the world. I had no idea what three weeks at sea would be like, but three weeks with a bunch of hot surfers and awesome waves? I was frothing. There was talk Kelly would be on it, but he couldn't make it. The crew was the full maniac crowd: Tom Carroll, Ross Clarke-Jones, Strider Wasilewski, Braden Dias and Dave Dixon.

I was so looking forward to surfing well and improving my surfing. After four days, I'd snapped my entire quiver. Every stick! I was riding these disposable little 5'10"s. They were paper-thin and the Mentawais just chewed them up. My back-up boards were Tom Carroll's! I had two and a half weeks riding Tom's heapas! It's the strangest feeling being unable to get good boards at a place like that. All you want to do is flare because the waves are amazing. But you're in a confined little space, seeing good waves going unridden and being surrounded by guys who just turn into animals. The anxiety was heavy. I thought I was going to die out there: sharks, getting smashed on the reef, I wasn't sure. In retrospect, I was a bit of a pussy. I think I could handle three weeks now, but I did get a bit intimidated by the whole thing.

The bigger waves had a lot of push. We were surfing this big scary left called Icelands. The captain said we were the first to surf it. A solid one came through and I didn't want it but I was called into it. I had to go, and it was a pretty sick wave. I was so stoked. That didn't stop them abusing me, though.

I was the youngest on the trip. Abuse is mandatory. I got hammered a couple of times. The last night was heavy. I was having a hell sleep. I'd just had the best surf and I was lying there, so content, thinking, "Yes! We're going home! How good's this!" Then in the early hours of the morning the animals boosted into my cabin. They grabbed me and I was kicking. I remember I booted Braden, then I got *so* smoked. They dragged me into the kitchen and threw food all over me. They were writing on me in texta. I had golden syrup in my ears and they covered me in every item from the fridge and pantry. I couldn't sleep so I sat up and they made me drink beer.

Tom: Taj was actually the same age as Dave Dixon. The contrast was Taj was the sheltered country kid and Dave was the only white guy at his school. Really streetwise. Dave instantly sided with us older guys and was saying stuff like, "What's Taj's trip? He should be stoked!"

His boards were a shocker. Poor guy, two and a half weeks without your owns boards. You want to perform. You could see it eating him. He broke one without even catching a wave, just paddling out and getting caught inside. That's a bit hard.

It was the most extraordinary trip I've ever been on for scoring. We surfed 26 breaks and named 17 of them. I guess it helped Taj to have us guys there, but he was all over everything anyway. It was obvious he was a complete natural. He got this incredible backside tube at Icelands on the big day and threaded the thing with such style.

Three weeks on a boat is a long time. We were going crazy. We'd been watching that Jack Nicholson movie *A Few Good Men*, about the young lawyer in the navy and the decorated general weeding out the pussies in the recruits. When someone brought the team down, they'd call "Code Red" on them. We'd called Code Red on Taj a few times but there was nothing too serious. On the last night, Taj was missing. He'd gone off to bed early. It was an obvious Code Red. We busted into his room, manned a station each (arm or leg) and taped his arms behind his back, taped his mouth and ankles together. He put up a good fight and kicked Braden, which snapped Braden into gear. We dragged him up to the galley table and smothered him in everything we could find. I think we freaked him out a bit so to let him know it wasn't a grommet thing, we worked Jeff Hornbaker, the photographer. It's a lot different with grommets today. Tying groms to poles in the nude was an everyday occurrence. It's weird now. Everyone helps grommets. Everyone is understanding. The get-out-of-here-learn-for-yourself mentality is gone. And that's kinda sad. It's a part of surfing.

TB TIP

FREEWHEELING. Don't wear tweeds or boxers under your wetsuit or trunks. No need. They don't add warmth nor aid comfort. Rattled by a small package? Don't be. Even if you've got a massive prong, your gear will hang down. And if you're playing the small prong blues in trunks, don't worry. No one can see your barb when you surf and when you're walking up the beach, position your prong behind the chunky fly.

B

WETSUITS

A

IF SOMEONE ASKED ME TO SPORT A TIGHT, FULL-LENGTH BODY SUIT MADE OF LYCRA, I'D PROBABLY TELL THEM THAT THEIR FLOAT AT THE GAY MARDIS GRAS WOULD BE APPEARING WITHOUT ME ON IT. THING IS, I NEVER QUESTION OR FEEL EMBARRASSED ABOUT SPRUIKING A SIMILAR ITEM MADE OF NEOPRENE.

Wetsuits. They make surfing in cold water possible. The smell of a brand-new one is more than enough to make you want to throw a week's wages over the counter. The surf's better in winter. Go through the heartache of icy feet, wet wetsuits and ice-cream headaches and you'll be better for it. SUIT YOURSELF...

▶ Okay, here's a few things you should know. Wetsuits are not supposed to be water tight. Their aim is to let a little bit of water in and trap it between rubber and skin. Your body temperature warms it, you stay warm and voila! you're surfing in winter, brudda. If you're still growing, buy a little bigger suit. To fill it out, wear a rashie underneath. But if your suit fits, you don't need a rashie.

▶ There's a whole variety of suits. I tend to steer clear of short johns and spring suits. I'm used to wearing long boardies, so I feel almost nude in a springie, with my pins exposed above the knee. It's just a personal thing but when it gets warm enough, I go from a short-arm steamer to boardies with a long-sleeve vest. Sweet.

▶ Your new suit will come with instructions about keeping it in good condition, but here's a rundown. (I'm not saying I do all of these things. Actually I do very few, but if it means you'll get another season from your suit, then it's been worth it.)

▶ Don't pee in 'em. Yeah, you'll warm up and, yeah, it's a pleasant sensation on a cold day, but it rots the neoprene. Not much water gets let into wetsuits, so not much gets out. It'll really stink up your suit.

▶ Rinse it in fresh water after a surf. Also, dry it inside-out and in the shade. This'll protect the outside so you'll still look good and it'll keep the rubber soft. Chlorinated pools are no good as well. Suits are soft and flexible when they're new. You're trying to maintain that.

▶ This one really sucks: hot water makes suits lose their flexibility and softness. It hurts, but jump in the cold shower, get that thing off then lord it up under that heat.

▶ Don't leave 'em baking in a hot car. It stinks out the car and wrecks the suit.

▶ If you're walking around after a surf with the suit pulled down to your waist, be sure to have the arms pulled out the right way. Otherwise the velcro from the neck will pill up the legs and neck area of the suit. Stick that velcro down whenever possible.

▶ When you're storing your suit in summer, sprinkle a little talcum powder over it. When winter rolls around, your suit will have retained plenty of flexibility and softness.

▶ Wax may rub onto the chest of your suit. Labels sometimes say you can clean it off, but I've found it pretty tough. You're not meant to use soap on 'em. You might be able to struggle with a scrubbing brush but you might also damage the suit. Besides, the wax will be straight back on after the next surf anyway. Not much you can do about this one.

▶ Sandy suits are torture. When you're getting out of your suit at the beach, get changed out of your suit on the rocks or grass rather than the sand. Or take it to the water's edge and rinse it off.

▶ Wet wetsuits. Changing into a freezing-cold suit on a dark winter morning is a fact of life for surfers. Avoid it by hanging your suit up the day before. If you've forgotten, though, just deal with it. It's the ripping off the plaster theory: the quicker you do it, the better. Think of it as a head start. Your mates haven't felt the shock of the cold yet. When they hit the water, they'll all be gingerly wading in while you, acclimatised, are paddling straight into the line-up to pick up the first wave. The other problem of a wet wetsuit is it is hard to get on. Put plastic bags over your feet and it will slip on with ease.

▶ The eighties and early nineties were all about brightness: white, fluro, multi-colours, whatever caught the eye. But, functionwise, colours don't make even one filthy lick of difference. Colour is there for fashion. Black is the go if you're trying to play it cool, especially if you're at a break full of locals. Also, if you've got a chick watching from the beach and you're putting in a woeful performance, chances are she won't be able to pick you out anyway.

▶ Don't get talked into buying a suit that doesn't work for you. If, like me, you don't like your pins hanging out, don't get talked into a spring suit. Same with colours.

▶ **Technicalities. Here's some stuff you should know...**

Blind stitched: the basic seam. If you're buying a major brand, this'll be standard. Sealed: seams doubled with glue. Taped and glued: all of the above, and taped as well, making the seams pretty much waterproof.

Booties, gloves and hoods. In extremely cold water, like in Victoria, Northern California, South Africa, Tassie, you're gonna need more than a standard steamer (full suit). For booties, get the thick, cold-water ones, not the thin, low-ankle ones made for walking over Indo reefs. No one wears those crook webbed paddling gloves anymore, but if you're surfing the really crazy-cold parts of the world, gloves are OK. Anything to keep warm.

The numbers. These refer to the thickness of the rubber in millimetres. 4/3 is four millimetres on the back and chest, three on the arms, legs and joints. And on, and on.

TB TIP

TAKE-OFF. When your boards are weighed at the airport, hold your foot under the end. You can easily make it 20 pounds lighter, which might save you excess baggage. Also, always wear a collared shirt when you check-in, and ask for a business-class upgrade. You've got no chance in a T-shirt. Your chances are slim, but if you don't ask, it won't happen. Alternatively, ask for an empty row, an aisle seat (easy to get to the bathroom) or one behind the emergency exit, where there's more leg room.

local beachie session w/ snake

airs looks sick when tail
is higher than nose
the more tail height the better.

looking down for
/ soft landing.

` my usual 4
finger homer
simpson hand.

— my house
(with mace in garage)

feeling comfortable and confident
in a steamer.
more padding if you stack it.

i love looking at somebody riding
a wave from the back when they disappear.
then punt one/

soft landing?

GWs looks Sick when tail
is higher than nose
(with mace in garage)

Feeling comfortable and confident
in a steamer.
more paddling if you stack it.

i love looking at somebody riding
a wave from the back when they disappear.

A. (FROM LEFT) TAJ WEARS A STEAMER (FULL SUIT) WHILE FIDDLING WITH FIGS, THE LONG-SLEEVED SPRING SUIT, THE SHORT-SLEEVED SPRING SUIT, THE WRESTLING SUIT AKA THE SHORT JOHN AND THE LONG-SLEEVED VEST. B. WETSUITS ARE FUTURISTIC CATSKINS – LOOSE AND WARM AND SENSUAL. GET ONE AND YOU'LL LAUGH IN THE FACE OF WINTER.

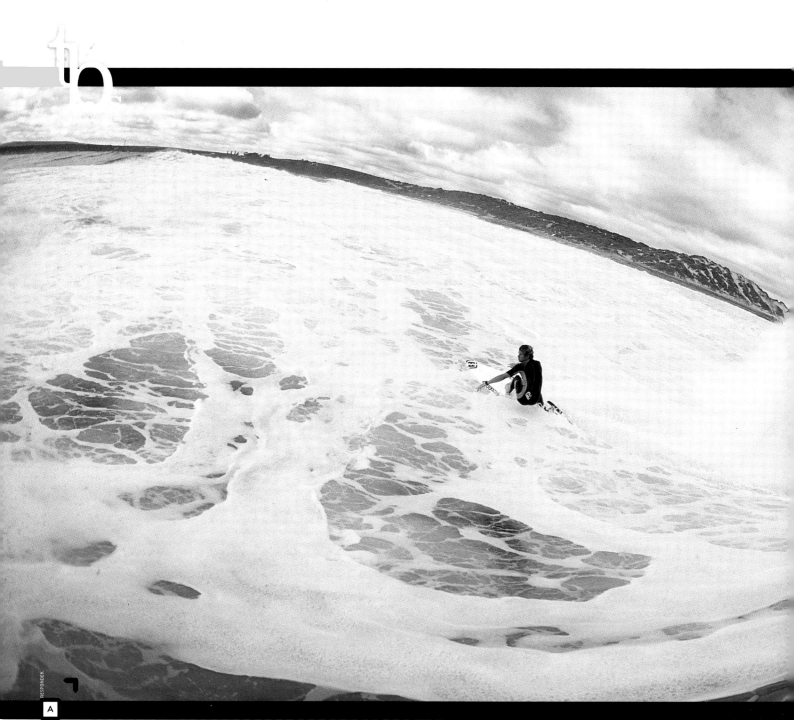

A. THIS PHOTO PROVES WHY GOOD STYLE IS ABOUT MUCH MORE THAN JUST LOOKS. CHECK IT OUT: TEEBS HAS HIS WEIGHT ON THE FRONT FOOT FOR DRIVE (BACK-FOOT IF HE'D WANTED TO PIVOT STRAIGHT AT THE LIP) WHILE THE REST OF HIS BODY - HEAD, TORSO AND ARMS - ARE ALL TWISTING AND SWINGING IN UNISON AS HE POWERS INTO IT. A PERFECT ILLUSTRATION OF FORM MEETING FUNCTION. B. EIGHT HOURS IN THE SURF MEANS YOU CAN EAT ICE-CREAM, DRINK BEER AND YOU WON'T GAIN AN INCH OF GIRTH.

BOTTOM TURNS

IT'S BEEN SAID BEFORE: A GOOD BOTTOM TURN SETS YOU UP FOR THE WHOLE WAVE. IT'S TRUE. BUT WHAT HASN'T BEEN SAID OFTEN ENOUGH IS THAT A BAD BOTTOM TURN WASTES THE WAVE.

You wind up digging a rail, get stuck in the turn, and just keep bottom turning off the wave, or you spin out and land on your ass under the lip. Either way, the section you looked so keen to annihilate goes off without you. It's embarrassing.

There's one other good reason to nail bottom turns. The part of the wave

where you do them, right out in front of the wave as it's pitching, is so smooth. As the water is drawn up into the wave, the lumps and bumps disappear. That means you can seriously lay into it.

SWING LOW...

▶ Drop straight down the face and look across at the section ahead. You want to time your bottom turn as late as possible, but not so late that the next section breaks on your head. So get your timing right. The best time generally is just as the lip is about to throw. That's when you're still fanging from the drop and the water coming at you is fast and smooth.

▶ When you're still learning, crouch low so you can make amends for any little mistakes. As you get better you will learn to stand a bit taller to do a quick move into the pocket, or crouch low for a long, way-out-in-front carve. On your forehand, lean over your toes, tweak your ankles and get into it. Sink your front shoulder and twist your back forward to keep your momentum. Keep your head up, looking at the section you're gonna hit. On your backhand, crouch and twist your shoulders to get things started. Look up to where you wanna go and swing your arms for-

ward as you power into it. Whichever way you're going, front-foot pressure is gonna give you drive to speed out into the face. Back foot pressure will pivot you into the pocket.

▶ As you get better, you'll learn to deliberately make your bottom turns more intense. Stand tall as you drop down the face, get a good look at the section ahead, then fade (just an ankle tweak will do it) towards the whitewater. This puts you into a more critical spot so you can lay even harder into it. Also, as you're going slightly the wrong way, you have to jam it even more.

▶ How hard you jam it depends on what you're gonna do next. Are you just fanging down the line, going for a reo or pulling into a barrel? If it's a reo, don't lean so much that you bury your rail and can't change direction halfway up the face. If you're fanging down the line or into a barrel, just know how much speed you want and keep your eyes where you wanna go.

▶ You can practice bottom turns all the time. Approaching a closeout and thinking about pulling off? Don't. Do a little bounce off the top and drop down the face. There might not be any wave left, but you've still got speed to lean into a bottom turn and then dive under the whitewater. You're not committed to do a move. There's no loss. Also, it'll ready you for kicking through sucky waves when a tube closes out or you're approaching a section of doom. If you just dive off in these places you can wear a lip to the head or leave your board in that zone that loves to break them. And for you contest frothers, it's

pretty cool to whack a closeout in a heat, come down and kick under the wash. Leaves a good image in the judge's minds and you're not groveling around in the whitewash.

▶ Some of the worst waves around give you a chance to try the best bottom turns, too. If you're surfing a beachbreak and it's onshore, sometimes you'll see a set wave that kind of doubles up – a bit at the top that throws long before the wave hits the bank. This gives you the chance for an easy drop down the face before the whole thing sucks up. Wait for it to break, and lay into your turn. Sure, you're going to cop a beating, but it's worth it just for those few seconds of sheer power turning.

TB TIP

HUH? GOOD FOOD? GIRTH? As you hit your twenties different fears take over: girth, baldness, excessive hair on the rig. Right here I'm talking girth. If you've surfed all day like I have here in Indo, eat what you want, drink what you want. If you're ever allowed pleasures, then that's when you've earnt it.

02

03

05

webber

globe

PHOTOS: RESPONDEK

A

A. DESPITE SURFING'S APPARENT RICHES, PRO'S LIKE TAJ ARE STILL A FEW YEARS AWAY FROM AFFORDING MAN SERVANTS TO AFFIX THEIR DECK GRIP AND STICKERS. B. THROWING THE FINS ABOVE THE LIP KEEPS 'EM OUTTA THE SAND.

AFFIXING A TAILPAD

IT WAS WEIRD. I HADN'T EVER USED A TAILPAD, HARDLY EVEN KNEW WHAT ONE WAS, WHEN A FRIEND I BARELY KNEW GOT ME A TAILPAD FOR MY SEVENTH BIRTHDAY. HIS MUM MUST'VE KNOWN I LIKED SURFING AND THEY GAVE ME THE OLD BARTON LYNCH THREE-DOT SPECIAL.

I took all the wax off an old 6'3" heapa and put this pad on and was turning all the dials of the direction of the grip making sure the grip was going the right way. More than 15 years later, I can't surf without them. If I do I just slip off the back and nail my shin because I'm so used to the kick on the tail. To be honest, I think the tail of a board looks so much better without them, the way the tail looks when it cuts through the water. Aesthetics aside, you need one. Here's why...

▶ Protection. Along with the nose, tails are the thinnest part of your board. The weight of your backfoot often blows out the tail. These are the worst dings ever. Tailpads provide extra protection and can help rid your board of these cancerous dings. They also help when duckdiving, which often means pushing your knee into your board. A pad softens the blow.

▶ Knowledge. When you stand up you instantly know if your feet are in the right place. If your pad has an arch, it'll also ensure your back foot is over the stringer. Something less to think about while you wonder what to do to that section just ahead.

▶ Performance. You want to do a frontside hack or an air, you can lock your foot in against the kick. If you've got wax, there's nothing to lock against.

AND HERE'S HOW TO PUT THEM ON...

▶ At 20 to 30 bucks, pads are too expensive to lose. And make no mistake, they do come off. If you're spiffing up an old board with a new pad, make sure you get every bit of wax off first. Otherwise, you'll soon find your new pad floating next to you in the line-up. Here's how: use a wax comb to get rid of the bulk wax. Use a cloth and elbow grease to get rid of the rest (hot water can help, too). Tough work but it'll mean you won't soil your board with chemicals. To make the surface better to adhere to, scratch it up with a little sandpaper. A new pad can pull an old board out of a rut.

▶ Even on a new board, you have to work to ensure your pad stays on. When you stick it down, rub it intensely, almost until your hands burn. There is nothing – nothing! – worse than feeling your tailpad come up and surfing on a board without grip.

▶ Timing. Once you lay the tailpad down, be committed. Don't rip the gear up if it isn't perfect, no one will notice. Once it's down, rub the entire surface so you generate a little heat. The heat will melt the glue and it'll never come up. Leave it for 24 hours before you ride on it.

▶ Positioning. Depends on your personal choice, but the further back you put it the safer you'll be. If it's too far back it's no big deal, but too far forward and you put your foot behind it, which is torture. I put it just in front of my plug. If the plug is too far forward, I'll cut a little hole in it so I can still get to the leash string.

▶ Reusing the gear. This is tough but it can work. The grip's own traction won't do much and you'll need to use some kind of crazy super glue kinda gear. But if you ever want to get the pad off again, it'll leave some serious gunk.

▶ Rash. If you're not used to using tailpads, you will get rashed. Just put up with it for a little while and you'll get used to it.

▶ Finally, a hit prediction. The full deck grip that was so popular in the eighties will make a comeback. You wait...

TB TIP

YOUR FINS DON'T DIG SAND. Don't let your fins drag through the sand too much when you're in the shallows because that may be enough to snap a fin out.

A

A. EARLY ON, YOU'LL RELY ON BACK-FOOT PRESSURE TO MAKE THE TURN. AS YOU GET BETTER, YOU'LL START LEANING FORWARD TO GET DRIVE. TB SHOWS HOW. B. A NEW BOARD WITH A TAILPAD THROWN IN FOR FREE. DOES IT GET ANY BETTER?

BASIC TURNING

BIG BOARDS ARE THEY KEY HERE. YOU DON'T HAVE TO WORK TO GET SPEED, YOU JUST GLIDE OVER TO THE PART OF THE WAVE WHERE YOU WANNA LAY DOWN YOUR FIRST TURN. OH YEAH, NOW YOU'RE GETTING TO THE GOOD BIT.

You might have caught a few waves and think you're doing the funnest thing in the world, but things are all only gonna get better. Think about it! Spray! From your rails! Top turns! Maneuvers! Let's do it.

YOUR TURN...

▶ You'll want to start by going frontside. It's genetic. You're facing the wave, you can see what's going on.

▶ Let's start with a bottom turn. Paddle into the wave aiming for the beach. Don't forget those extra couple of hard strokes, and jump up. Turning is all about pointing your body and looking where you want to go. When you've made the drop, look across the green face and lean over your toes. Point with your front arm. The higher you point, the harder you turn. How's it feel? Pretty good, huh? The first thing you'll notice is that you are using the water rushing up the face of the wave, and if you don't pull out of the turn, you'll just get blown over the back of the wave. Later, you will learn to tweak your ankles to turn your board. Just a little push from them will get your board turning where you want it to go. But for now, keep them fairly rigid and get the feel of your weight doing all the work.

▶ So you're on the face, or at least not at the bottom of the wave, and you need to get back down. What you are about to attempt now is the humble beginnings of a cutback. Again, look where you want to go, which now is back to the bottom of the wave. Swing your front arm back behind your body, and move your weight to your heels,

mainly your back one. Hopefully, your shoulders and hips will also turn. If not now, they will eventually. All these combinations become instinctive after a while. Bend your legs a bit too. This gives you a bit of leeway when things go wrong, so you don't fall.

▶ If you make the turn back down, twist your body and look back up the wave to do it again. Don't get flustered if you're falling. You will. If you nose-dive as you roll down the face you need more weight on your back foot. Same applies if you turn but your board does not. Give it more back foot pressure.

▶ If you hit a dead section of the wave, do some bunny hops (bouncing on the board and pushing harder on your front foot as you come back down). This squirts water through the tail, generating speed.

▶ When you get better at paddling, you can avoid the need for a bottom turn. As the wave approaches, simply point your board down the line and let the wave push you along it.

▶ Eventually, you'll get a glimpse of spray coming off your rails. Don't forget, the gig is to look where you're going, not at your feet to see how much water you're moving. But, having said that, those first few glimpses of spray are pretty magical. When you see it fanning from your rail, you'll think there's not a better sight in the world.

▶ Give it a few months, and you'll be doing it with speed and spontaneity in more critical parts of the wave. But first, you need to...

Go backside!

Riding backside puts your back to

the wave. It's a rattle at the start, but later you'll do it without thinking. Your first backside turns are far easier than your frontside ones because you have to twist your body. You're pivoting from the moment you stand up. What you will soon learn is this: a backside bottom turn is the same motion as a frontside cutback. Likewise, a backside top turn is essentially a frontside bottom turn. Master one, master both. So now, to get back to the bottom of the wave, make like a frontside bottom turn: crouch, lean over your toes, look where you wanna go, and cruise on down.

TB TIP

DON'T ASK, DON'T GET. Boards are expensive. So, when you're buying, ask for a better rate or an added bonus. Pair of shoes... "free socks?" New board... "Leash and tail-pad?" Something smaller... "Block of wax?" Better still, buy a new steamer, some racks, or whatever else you might need at the same time, and get a deal for the lot.

01

03

05

A

B

A. EVEN WHEN IT'S SMALL YOU CAN STILL THROW YOUR WEIGHT AROUND. B. BIG BOARDS TEACH YOU TO DRAW STRONG LINES.

BASIC TURNING

02

06

A. THE FOAM: NOT TOO THREATENING, MORE PREDICTABLE AND THE TANKS LOVE TO DRIVE THROUGH IT. B. PUNTING WITH THE CONFIDENCE OF A RELIGIOUS LEASH-WEARER.

WHITEWASH TURNS

I WOULDN'T NORMALLY RIDE A TANK LIKE THIS BUT WHEN I WAS DOING THE SHOTS, IT WAS COOL BECAUSE IT SLOWED DOWN MY SURFING AND HELPED ME TAKE IN A FEW OF THE SUBTLETIES OF TURNING.

Whitewash is good for learning. It pushes you along, and you can ease into your turns. The photos do the most of the talking here, so I'm gonna chill on the words, okay?

WASHING UP...

▶ Whitewash, whitewater, foam – whatever you want to call it, it's pretty forgiving. It's your friend because it gives you the chance to do turns beyond your ability.

▶ Okay, say you can move up and down the wave face but you haven't yet pulled off what you could call a proper turn. The whitewash will help you lay down some legit gear.

▶ What's the difference between a whitewater section and any other section? Whitewater sections spill more than throw and are usually on fat waves. The opposite is real sucky surf, where the waves are barreling. There's a million kinds of waves in between and no session will ever have just one or the other. If you're learning, though, you'll more than likely be getting amongst the whitewater.

▶ So you're moving across a wave on your forehand. You know how to move up the face by looking at the top of the wave and by lifting your front arm. So do it as the breaking section approaches.

▶ Keep the weight on your back foot as you move up the face and apply weight on your front foot as you hit the section.

▶ Because it's not sucky, the aim is that the section will fling you back down in front of the wave. Relax. Let the wave do the work for you.

▶ Likewise, if you're learning to do proper top turns, the wash is the go because it's there to knock your board back down the face.

▶ Later, all you'll want is steep sucky waves because they give you more options to tear out your full artillery of maneuvers. But even when you become more advanced you'll still love the foam to get jiggy with. You can race toward it and waft some fin, throw down a layback or knock out a reverse. And here's the best bit: falling off in it hardly ever means you cop a beating.

TB TIP

LEASHLESS IN SEATTLE? I think I'm the only person in the world who doesn't like surfing without a leash. Everyone says surfing without one is like sex without a condom – heightens sensitivity and all that crap. I hate it. I fall off 99 per cent of the waves I catch. If you're not falling, you're not pushing yourself. It's the most stupid thing I could ever think of. You have to deal with blowing a wave and then you have to deal with swimming to the beach to get your board! But then, I've seen Pat O'Connell ride four-foot closeouts in a heat and never lose his board. So if you really wanna surf without a leash, don't do it in crowded surf and don't do it if there's any rocks on the beach. Even if there's just the tiniest cluster, your board will be drawn to it like a magnet.

01

A

TB AT A FAVORITE OFFSHORE BEACHBREAK IN QUEENSLAND. DIG ON THE BLACK T-SHIRT, TAJ'S PREFERRED ALTERNATIVE TO RASHIES. WHY? RASHIES LOOK RANK.

FEELING THE GROOVE

If you get a surfboard for Christmas and think that by February you're going to be diving into this section, then I don't want to be the wet blanket. You're taking on the world's most difficult sport. Don't believe me? Okay, if you persisted for ten years at learning the guitar, horse riding, even studying to be a doctor you'd get to a fairly decent level of expertise. You could surf for ten years and never really get it. Twenty bucks doesn't buy you time on the court to practice over and over. The surf is crowded and then you've got to find a wave that works for you. Train maneuvers, let alone a similar section to let you perfect them. But without challenges life is a series of worthless events and this book is here to challenge the challenges. And by now you're probably infected. How good is this?

YOUR FIRST TUBE

CALL IT WHAT YOU LIKE — BARREL, SHACK, CAVE, PIT OR GREEN ROOM. IT IS THE BEST THING IN SURFING. AS A SURFER, THIS IS WHAT YOU LIVE FOR. I CAN'T IMAGINE ANYTHING FEELING BETTER. ONCE YOU TASTE IT, YOU WILL HUNT IT FOR THE REST OF YOUR LIFE. WORK? SCHOOL? RESPONSIBILITIES? THEY'RE NOTHING IF THERE ARE BARRELS TO BE HAD.

Don't worry, it's not just you. Something special happens in there. I used to think I had had heaps of tubes until one day when I was around 11 or 12 my dad filmed me. I was thinking I was getting all these sick little tubes, then I went home to check out the video evidence. The truth was cruel. I was absolutely nowhere near the tube! I remember thinking, "Whoa, I have really got to park it." To save you the same embarrassment, here's some tips about the tube.

PULLING IN...

▶ The best way to practice getting tubed is to pull into frontside closeouts (backside is much harder, and we'll get to that later). Make sure the wave is throwing, not crumbling.

▶ This time, you're not looking where you're going, you're looking up at the lip. It's a whole new ball game. All your movements will be in response to what that lip does.

▶ The head dip blues. You may think that because your face and head are under the lip, you're steaming through in perfect style. You're not. You're just in the pocket. Nice feeling, but not a barrel.

▶ Keep your legs bent when looking for the barrel. Sure, you've seen photos of hot surfers standing tall in the barrel, but slow down, tiger, you're learning. Besides, your first few barrels are not going to be that big.

▶ Stay directly over your board. Can't emphasize this one enough, really.

▶ Don't freak out. Don't close your eyes in the tube. Ever. I know you're only new to this game and used to spending a good deal of time falling but a lot of the time virgin pit riders miss tubes because they've got their eyes closed. Also, don't give up. Always try to ride that barrel as long as you can. If you jump, it's only because you're afraid of falling off. Don't jump, and you increase your chance of not falling. Just because you're inside the wave doesn't mean you're toast.

▶ Setting up the tube. When you're in sucky waves, practice setting up barrels by staying in the pocket. Keep a low center of gravity, and get a feel for this part of the wave. It's intense, and unforgiving. Run your hand along the face of the wave and get used to the feeling of riding high and low.

▶ Waves that barrel are typically steeper and harder to take off on. Some give you an easy drop before building and pitching, in which case you'll have to stall or slow down to get in it. But most barrels are straight after a steep take-off. If you're paddling into a wave that looks like it's going to throw, paddle hard. Your last stroke is like a mini-maneuver, setting your speed and position for the barrel. If it's a fast barrel and you struggle with the drop, the tube will leave you behind. Lean forward as you stand up, take a quick look at the wave's face, which is where you're heading, then look up to the lip.

▶ I've hinted that your ankles are crucial to good surfing. Well, in the barrel, they are everything. You don't want to move your body around too much inside because you'll get clipped by the lip. So to make adjustments in your line, tweak your ankles. You can even generate speed by using them to pump your board. The other adjustment you can make is to drag your arm in the wave face to slow yourself down.

▶ The biggest thing is to identify which waves barrel. Only experience can teach you that. But don't worry, once you have tasted tuberiding, you will dedicate your life to experiencing it whenever you can. After that, it's working out how deep you can get. You may think I'm crazy, but play the surf game on PS2. This is really what setting up the tube is like.

▶ Oh yeah, and as for Gerry Lopez's famous statement that the safest part of the wave is in the tube, he's right. I guess. Just try to ignore the horror stories on pages 120 and 150.

TB TIP

TARPING UP. "You're only the second person I've ever slept with." Stop flattering yourself, stupid. You've been sucked in. Unprotected sex is dumb. God knows, we're all guilty but for the sake of a little more enjoyable rutting, tarp up. Terminations, kids and STDs are not good. Gotta wear the chimmey chongers.

A

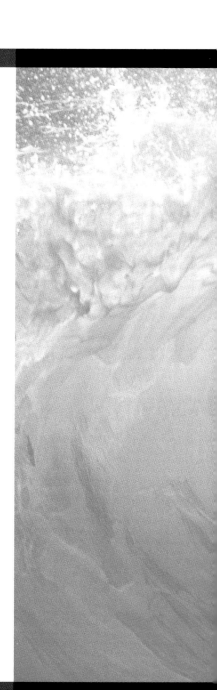

B

A. A WEEPING PRONG IS NOT A LAUGHING MATTER, NOR IS SIRING A CHILD AT 18. B. THE FIRST TIME YOU GET TUBE VISION, WHEN THE CURL OF THE WAVE FOLDS IN FRONT OF YOUR FACE, IS THE DAY ALMOST EVERYTHING ELSE WILL CEASE TO MATTER.

A

A. GOOD SLASHES WILL MAKE YOU FEEL SUPERHUMAN AS YOU STUFF THAT TAIL IN THE POCKET AND SHOWER THE HEAVENS WITH SPRAY. B. TEEBS AND A 400 FOOTER AT PIPE.

ON THE FACE SLASH

ARE YOU READY TO FEEL THE GROOVE? TO FEEL THE CURVE OF THE WAVE, AND THE POWER IN YOUR BOARD? COOL. LET'S DO AN ON-THE-FACE SLASH THEN.

By now, you can do whitewash floaters and basic face turns. You're starting to get the feel of your board beneath your feet, and this sensitivity allows you to make some pretty sharp transitions.

▶ The best thing about the open-face slash is that it's one of the few turns you can do without a lot of speed. That's the reason it exists. You don't have enough speed to do a big carve off the top of the wave but you're in the pocket and you want to take advantage of the section.

▶ All turns feel good and it's better to be turning than to be doing nothing, so this is a good one when there's not much happening on the wave. It can also be a speed turn as you're racing down the line. You see a section approaching that you want to hit, but before you get there you want to squeeze in a little turn that doesn't burn all your speed. The open-face slash is your answer.

▶ You need a wave with a decent gradient – anything steeper than, say, 45 degrees. You can do the slash anywhere you like on the face, but the higher you hit it the better it looks. Do it on the bottom, and the wash will hit you quickly and you probably won't be able to come out of the turn with any speed or grace. You'll find yourself stinking it up in the whitewater.

▶ Aim high and do a reasonably committed bottom turn diagonally up the face. No use trying to bottom turn hard and hitting the lip because you don't have enough speed, and remember you may be trying to get two turns out of this wave.

▶ Bottom turn with most of the weight on the balls of your feet, more on the back one than the front. At the same time spread your wings so you've something to release when you get to the top of the wave. Your arms do all the work, so you have to get them ready for action.

▶ When you move up the face, your weight should be evenly distributed over your feet and you should be looking at the section you hope to pivot on.

▶ When you reach the top of the wave, look back to the bottom. Really plant your back foot and stay centred over your board. Push with about 80 per cent of your power (too much, and you'll spin out). Use your arms to restrict the move. If this was a full cutback, you'd be swinging your whole upper body round, but this maneuver is just a little snap before you continue on down the line. Keep your shoulders square, and your hands pointing roughly along the wave. Stay crouched to let your body absorb the turn. Sometimes, if you're a bit unsteady, you can put your back arm in the whitewater to stop you falling off.

▶ After the turn, your fins will take a moment to find their line again. So don't go into the next turn too quickly. It has happened to me a lot. I've been in control, standing there, looking toward the next section, gone straight into a bottom turn and, because my board isn't ready, fallen flat on my face.

▶ If all goes well, another section will be waiting for you to climb straight up onto. And if you were just doing a speed turn before the main event, you'll approach it with speed and firmly planted feet.

TB TIP

HOW BIG? Calling wave size. When a six-foot-tall surfer catches a six-foot wave, the wave is far bigger than head high. When a six-foot dude catches a double overhead wave, it is not 12 feet. And when a wave is six foot high from behind, it does not necessarily mean it's six foot. It's a confusing, macho and stupid, but accepted, way of judging wave size. You can't really explain it until you spend enough time around people who surf. You kinda just work out what a six-foot wave is, what a four-foot wave is. It's just the average from all the crap you've heard over the years. The safest bet is to call wave size based on a person's personal landmarks eg. Ankle high, waist height, shoulder high, head high, overhead, double overhead, triple overhead and so on. Incidentally, *Surfer* magazine recently started describing waves by their literal height, and it is becoming widely accepted. A wave that is six feet high is called six foot. Be interesting to see if it lasts.

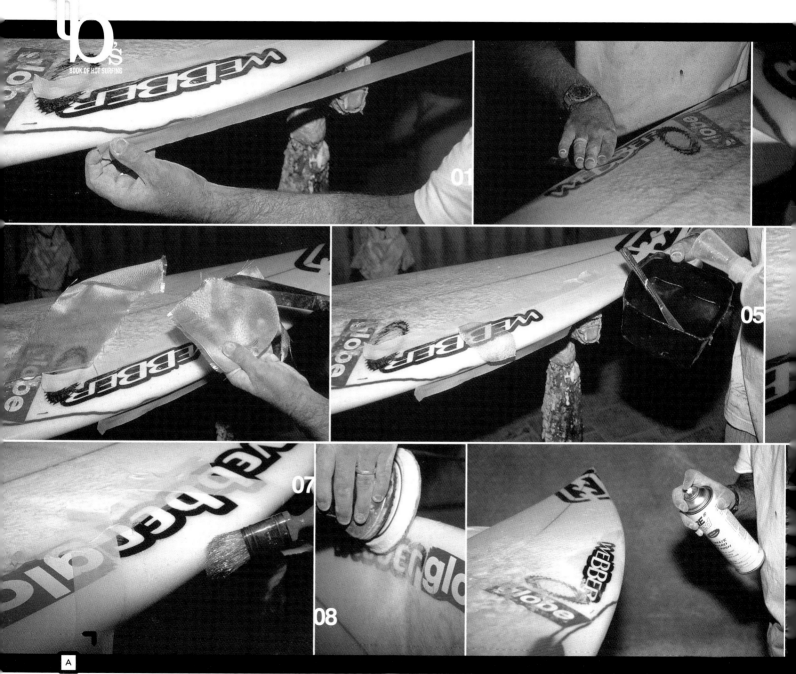

01

05

07

08

A

A. YOUR FIRST DING FIX IS A TOWERING ACHIEVEMENT. BE PROUD BECAUSE YOU'RE ONE STEP CLOSER TO BEING THE COMPLETE SURFER. B. TEXTING AND CREEPINESS: TOO EASY.

FIXING DINGS

LEAVING DINGS IN YOUR BOARD IS A TICKET TO GRIEF. AN UNFIXED DING TAKES IN WATER, MAKING YOUR BOARD HEAVIER, WEAKER AND AN UGLY SHADE OF BROWNY YELLOW.

My advice? Fix dings as soon as you get 'em. Or in my case, get someone to fix 'em as soon as you get 'em. Twiggy, the man who I shoot photos with most of the time, is also my ding fixer. This is his method.

▶ Get a ding repair kit from a surf shop. It should contain some Q cell (white powder), sandpaper, a tin of resin, some fiberglass, a small jar of hardener (or catalyst).

▶ Dry the ding by leaving it in the sun for a few hours. But cover the rest of the board with a towel if you don't want it to turn an ugly colour.

▶ Rough up the surface around the ding using 80 grit sandpaper. Get rid of any shrapnel and any dead glass by ripping it with your fingers or a scalpel. This will give the new layer of glass something to stick to.

▶ Now, if it's a big ding, you need to fill it first with Q cell. If it's on the bottom or deck, place the board on a bench, ding up, and tape around it, say four inches from the hole, to prevent resin from running all over your board. If it's on the rail, place the board fins down on a bench, with the ding hanging over the edge. If the ground beneath needs protecting, lay some newspaper down. Then run tape along the rail so it cups the resin when you pour it in.

▶ Cut a piece of fibreglass to fit over the ding. These get a bit messy once they're soaked in resin, and don't always go on as planned, so have a few spare strips ready as well.

MIXING THE BREW...

There should be some instructions on the tin of resin about how much catalyst to mix in. For a small ding, just a couple of drops is usually enough. Shake in a couple extra if it's a cold day. Careful, though. Put in too much and it will harden before you can get it on the board. And even if you do, it will be a bad job because the resin will be brittle. If it hardens too quickly, the mix will get hot and start smoking. Don't worry if this happens. It won't catch fire.

▶ If you've done a Q cell filler, wait till it dries and sand it back roughly to accommodate a layer of fiberglass on top. Now, mix another brew of resin. Place your fiberglass where you want it, and, using a paint brush, paint on the resin until the fiberglass is soaked. Fill up all the little gaps and press out any air bubbles. If there are any drips of resin on your board, clean them off with a rag. If they dry, you'll have to sand them down later.

▶ There are two types of resin you can use but that will depend on how you get your resin. Ding repair kits (which are really good value) contain filler resin. This gives the board the best finish after you sand it. Or you can go to a board glasser and scrounge up some laminating resin, which is stronger, and a few off-cuts of fiberglass. You'll also have to buy filler resin because laminating resin dries sticky and needs filler resin on top to sand. So, say you use laminating resin, when it dries you need to paint on a layer of filler resin.

▶ Your resin's dry, you're now ready to sand. Pull up the masking tape, and again use 80 grit sandpaper to bring the ding down. Hand sanding with a block is a good way. Then decrease the abrasiveness of the sandpaper with lesser grits to get a better job. Say, 120 grit, then 240 grit. For a real super good finish, you can use the 600 grit wet and dry paper. Voila! Your board is as good as new!

TB TIP

WHY SMS IS YOUR BEST FRIEND. Text messages are the ultimate surf communicators. You can wake your mate without waking his whole family, do away with the idle chat, and get straight to the point: "4ft o/s, lo crowd, whr r u?" Typing text is more discreet, too. It doesn't look good to stand in the parking lot yelling to your mates down the line that it's going off. I only recently got reception at my house. Now I don't even use my home phone any more. I can't live without my mobat. I'm a text fiend.

A. TEEB MAKES A CLEAN JUMP, DESPITE BREAKING A FEW RULES. B. BE TIMID AND YOU'LL CATCH NOTHING. ATTACK!

THE ROCK JUMP

NO MATTER HOW WELL YOU KNOW A BREAK, NO MATTER HOW MANY TIMES YOU'VE JUMPED OFF THE ROCKS OR HOW EXPERIENCED YOU ARE, SOONER OR LATER YOU WILL GET LICKED. TRUST ME.

It's a big day at North Point, near my home. The sets are six-to-eight feet. I want to jump in at the bay on the inside, which means a long paddle all the way round the break, but Rictor (Rick Jakovich) takes me out to the spot at the edge of the rocks where the maniacs jump off. From there it's only a short paddle to the take-off zone. I've jumped from there before, but only on smaller days. It doesn't look bad, but it is. I'm rattled. The shelf you have to run across is really slippery. I check for sets, think everything is cool, and start to make my way across the ledge. And of course an eight-foot bomb comes outta nowhere. It's too slippery to run back. I'm stranded. I have no idea what to do. I kinda set up my footing as well as I can and try to jump over a mess of screaming Indian Ocean whitewater, and get hammered. Absolutely flushed. I get picked up and tossed 50 yards underwater, just waiting for my head to be planted into the rocks. I swear, I nearly end up in the bushes.

Rock jumps are heavy, but the sooner you realise your pretty skin is gonna take some damage, the sooner you can enjoy the pleasures of 'em. So, what are the pleasures? Well, dry hair and a short, untroubled paddle into the line-up, for a start. But, also, a well-timed rock jump is a cool move. You feel confident, and you're at the start of a session! You're ready to flare! Here, I'm going to tell you how to minimize the risk when jumping off rocks. I can't tell you where the barnacles are, or the safest jump spots. Hopefully, after reading this, you'll be able to work that out

for yourself. But I can tell you this: paddle from the bay at North Point.

LET'S ROCK...

▶ Never walk over boulders with sand on your feet. This gear is like soap on rocks. Wash the sand off in a rancid little pool of water on the way.

▶ Put your leash on before you leave the sand. This way, you don't have to put your precious board down on the hard, abrasive rocks. Hold your board on the same side as your leash, and hold the leash in that hand, keeping it fairly tight between your hand and your ankle. This prevents the leash getting caught on rocks. Don't let go until you jump in the water. If it's hanging loose when you jump, it can easily get caught and slingshot you back into the rocks at the worst possible time. If you're wearing a steamer, put your leash on the outside of your wettie, in case you have to rip it off in a hurry.

▶ Know the rocks. Some don't look real slippery, but are. Watch out for thin coverings of algae or seaweed, which can be like a thin film of oil. Also be careful of barnacles and sea urchins. If it's a popular jump spot, locals will have worked out the best path, right down to the individual rocks they step on. Look for their footprints or where the tops of the rocks have been worn smooth, free from moss or scum.

▶ The key, as usual, is confidence. Watch where other people jump, and how they time it. Do they stop before running across the ledge, or do they wait right at the edge? If they blow it, how many waves would it take to wash them back on the rocks? If the

answer is one, make sure you know what you're doing.

▶ Never turn your back on the ocean. And don't just look for sets 20 yards from the rocks. Look deep into the ocean. Look for dark lines and lumps.

▶ Never jump as a set is approaching. Know the rhythm of the sets. How many waves are they? How long are the lulls? This shouldn't take long to work out. Don't stand there thinking about what might go wrong. Once you've acquired the critical information, commit yourself. Standing there is only going to make you nervous. Plus, you might be holding up others who want to get to the jump spot. Hesitating does not look good. When you've got a lull, get to the spot where you can leap into deep water. Quickly check where the submerged rocks are, then wait for a little wave, and jump. You must time it as the wave is at its highest because its receding will wash you away from the rocks. You don't want to be near the rocks when the next wave hits, even if it's a little one.

▶ Sometimes you'll be stranded on the shelf with a wave approaching. Unless you can make it back to safer ground before it hits you, don't run away from it, or your feet will be bowled from under your body and you'll most likely get ploughed into the rocks. Look for the highest point you can reach, a rock you can shelter behind, or something to hang onto. Failing all that, you'll have to jump over it. Try to clear the front of it, then get swept up in the water behind. With a bit of luck, you'll only wind up in the bushes! Ha!

▶ Not all jump spots are perfect. Sometimes you'll be standing there with a wave approaching that you'll have to jump into, and realize there are rocks everywhere. You know this is not going to be a smooth move, or look elegant. Burleigh Point is a perfect example. The round, slippery rocks gently slope into the water so you never actually get to a jump spot. You just reach a point and go, "Okay, I hope it's good enough, because, damn, I gotta jump!" The good news is that the wave will cover the rocks and get you on clean water. Just go.

▶ The leap is easy. Lean forward, hold your board in front of you, and, with that leash still in your hand, go for it. Let go of the leash as you extend your body over the water. Pull your board under you and, whammo, you're ready to paddle. Go for it, and don't look back.

TB TIP

COLD? Offshore's biting through you? Sit in close, paddle hard, catch lots of waves. Surf like it's summer and you're wearing trunks. It'll warm you, body and soul.

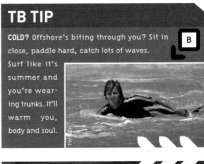

TWIGGY

HOW TO

TWO MONTHS IS WAY TOO LONG TO WAIT TO GET A NEW STICK. HERE'S HOW YOU CAN GET IT WAY SOONER...

Reader, I bow to the surfing expertise of Taj Burrow in all areas but one: getting a custom back from a shaper within a reasonable timeframe. You really think TB has to cough up five hundred skinnies and then grovel for his fiberglass? Ha! The world's best at the shaping game line up to hand him their wares, the incredible Greg Webber his current favorite.

So, you've got the coin, got the dimensions, how do you get your shaper to move on your order? Here's some tips.

1. Follow up the order with a phone call one week later. Ask if you can come and watch it be shaped. The shaper will hack up a lung in surprise and think, f**k, I better move on this one.

2. After it's been shaped, go visit the glasser. Tell him you'll spot him a case of beer if he'll push your board through. No one visits glassers. Mostly they are sad, lonely, unhealthy old men, all doomed to die of some hideous lung disease, sooner rather than later, on sweat-soaked beds in an underfunded hospice. Give them your attention and they're all yours.

3. Don't nail the shaper too hard on a deal. A full-price board will always get preference over the kid who talked his way into a $200 discount.

4. Never order a board from a shaper-to-the-stars if the tour's in town. All the shaper has eyes for during the exciting two weeks around a contest are pro surfers. Wait until all the fuss has died down, then move.

5. Don't go overboard with the spray. Artists are even more precious and work-shy than shapers. If your spray is too complex the shaped blank will sit in the spray racks for weeks while the sprayer develops the necessary inspiration.

6. Finally, don't overlook shapers whose star has begun to wane. The former hero is still as good as he always was and you have the benefit of his panic 'cause he knows his business is going down if he doesn't nail a few customs from ordinary guys.

TB TIP

THE RUN ROUND. Surffing is all about rhythm. Some days it'll be packed and you'll be on everything that breaks. Other days you'll be out of synch and watch perfect waves peel empty. If you're surfing a point, run don't walk. You keep your focus, your heart-rate up and you're back in the water with the same rhythm of the ocean. And when you walk around, there's that easy lure to just wrap the session then and there. Bolt, dammit. Bolt!

JACK ENGLISH

A

A. WHEN IT ALL COMES TOGETHER, CONFIDENT SURFING MEANS: LATE, FAST FIN-WAFTS AND AN EASY RIDE UP THE BEACH ON THE SHOULDERS OF FRIENDS. TB OPENS UP WHILE BRUCE IRONS PRETENDS HE'S NOT LOOKING. B. THE RESULT OF CONFIDENCE? THE CHAIR UP THE BEACH AND THE NOVELTY CHECK. C. REIGNITE THE FLAME WITH SOME VIRTUAL MIND MOVES.

SURFING WITH CONFIDENCE

THIS IS A WEIRD PIECE OF WISDOM BUT I'M GOING TO TRY TO TELL YOU HOW TO SURF WITH CONFIDENCE. THING IS, IF I REALLY KNEW, I'D BE RATED NUMBER ONE IN THE WORLD FOR THE NEXT DECADE.

It's an early round of the Rip Curl Cup, at Sunset. I've got an easy heat, and I'm not even slightly nervous. I get a good wave, sniff out a tube through the sketchy inside bowl, lay down a cuttie and rack up nine points. Sorted. Now all I need is a two-point ride to get an easy lead and I've got half the heat to find it. To earn two points from the judges, all you need to do is take off, trim and do a little turn. Sometimes, just making the take-off is enough. It's not a challenge. I catch four waves, and can't even stand up! I get myself into an increasingly bad frame of mind until I can't even do the most basic thing in surfing. So I lose the heat. It's heavy. Then, when I'm walking up the beach, this cocky girl says, "Got wax, Taj?" I've never felt so dis-

appointed. But the flipside is when you're surfing well and your board feels good. That's when you're truly high on life.

LET'S SEE HOW IT HAPPENS...

▶ Feeling good and confident is all locked in your head. Confidence for me can simply mean I like the trunks or wetsuit I'm wearing, or I've got a cool deck spray or clean wax job.

▶ Remember that being a surfer means you are one of the luckiest people in the world. And if you live near the beach, have friends who surf there all the time, and get waves all year round, you are truly blessed. Remember that.

▶ I used to have bad surfs and get myself really pissed off. I'd turn on myself ridiculously for not linking my turns properly. I'd hate myself and think, "Look at yourself. You're a kook. You shouldn't be where you are!" I'd be in the water swearing and cursing. Then my dad would just pull my head in straight away, and say, "What the hell are you talking about? Have a good look at yourself, you little idiot." Someone smart once said, when you find yourself in a hole, stop digging.

▶ Your rhythm and confidence is infectious. Focus on the waves you're stinking up and you'll keep doing it. If I feel negativity creeping in, I just stop right there and turn it around. Start fresh. Breathe deeply. Remember, you're surfing, you're having fun. Totally block it out. Realize how lucky you are. Most people go their whole lives without surfing. Some people never even see the ocean. Think about that for a while. That fumbled take-off suddenly won't seem so bad any more.

▶ There will have been times when you were invincible. We all have them, no matter what level we're at. They are the sessions when every turn you attempt, you make, and everything falls into place. Think of those sessions.

Think of what was going through your head. The feel of the water, the sound of the waves. I think of a session I had at Rabbit Hill, in front of my house. I can picture how perfect it was, how amazing my board felt under my feet. I could drop into waves ridiculously late. I was paddling under the lip, spinning round, air-dropping into the tube and getting spat out clean. I was invincible.

▶ You would have seen guys who surf their home breaks really well, but who struggle away from it. It's hard to take the confidence of home away with you. I've tried. Rabbit Hill is like Backdoor. But I'll never surf Backdoor as confidently. All I'm thinking is about the reef and what could go wrong. If only I could bluff myself into thinking I was at home. The battle would be won.

TB TIP

CONSOLE SURFING. Is real surfing getting a bit boring you? Bust out the PS2 and wait for the fire to ignite. Music.

A. CLEAN BOARDS FEEL GOOD AND FAST AND DRIVEY EVEN ON DARK DAYS. TAJ THROWS OUT THE FRONT ARM ABOVE THE HEAD AT LOWER TRESTLES IN CALIFORNIA, THE STABILIZER IN ANY TURN WITH THE POTENTIAL TO GO TO LAYBACK. B. WHO'D OF THOUGHT SOMETHING LIKE THIS WOULD BE THE BEST WAY TO CHECK THE SURF.

SEUSSING YOUR BOARD

I KNOW I SAID I LIKE THE FEEL OF BIG THICK UGLY WAX JOBS BUT I'M ALWAYS GETTING MY FIX OF CLEAN WHITE UNTOUCHED CRAFT. YOU'RE NOT. IF YOU'RE ONLY GETTING ONE BOARD A YEAR, OR EVEN A FEW, IT'S NICE TO KEEP THEM IN A WHITE, TIGHT CONDITION.

If you're talking longevity with your boards, there are some cleaning techniques to do it right. The first thing is to get dings fixed as soon as you get them.

TIGHT WHITE...

Getting rid of the wax from your board.

▶ To get rid of the bulk of the wax, use the beveled edge of your wax comb. Don't go pouring hot water on your craft or you'll risk a delam (cool speak for delamination). Five minutes in the sun will do the job, softens it right up. Then hit it with your comb. Cool kids and pros mostly use paint scrapers.

▶ You'll get most of the crap off your board but there'll be areas where the board's got pressure dings that'll be filled with wax. Two options here. The first is to get a towel or cloth and rub the gear off. The second is foam dust. You can grab a plastic bag and get it off the floor of your local shaper's shaping bay. Rub it into the small areas of wax and it'll come off. Make sure you do it on the grass. Inside and you'll really stink the place up.

What about the blemishes and the crap that won't come off?

▶ Surfboards are fairly complicated. The consumer: you, me and every other kid in the water likes their things shiny and well-presented. So, lacquer and all sorts of crazy coats go on our boards to make them look good. Start throwing round solvents and thinners and your board will lose these nice finishes.

▶ To clean your boards, use a rag and the household cleaners like the multi-purpose citrus kinda gear (Spray 'n Wipe) your mom's got under the sink. That should move most of the crap. If that doesn't work for the stubborn gear, hit it with Mr Sheen or a really fine-grade wet-and-dry sandpaper.

Okay, still there. Now what?

▶ If your board is yellow, no scrubbing is getting the thing white. The sun does to your boards what ciggies do to your pegs.

▶ And, I know what you're going to say. You used artline pens, Poscas and spray paint on your board and now you want to get rid of it, didn't you? Huh? Well, you've got no choice but to use the thinners. You should be able to get it clean (most boards have a lacquered finish so you can remove gunk) but you will lose that finish. It isn't too obvious though, so if you're over that spray like a crook tatt, lose it.

Isn't there gear designed specifically for taking it off?

▶ Yeah, there's products out there that do the same job but you're probably paying for the name. The good thing about them is that they don't use solvents, so it's peace of mind there's no chance of destroying your craft.

What about really buffing up my craft?

▶ This is a good 'un. Car polish. Throw it down in circular motions, then get a smooth, dry cloth and buff and shine your craft to perfection. Just make sure there are no cleaners left on your board when you hit the water. Your golden craft may be all lubed up. It's official, your board is seussed.

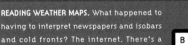

TB TIP

READING WEATHER MAPS. What happened to having to interpret newspapers and isobars and cold fronts? The internet. There's a crapload of sites ready to tell you when, how and what you're gonna score. Web cams, four-day forecasts, winds, tides, the lot. Punch in the beach or region you're interested in along with the words "surf check" and you're away.

B

CRYSTAL SIMPSON >

< JAY DAVIES

< ME

< KERBY BROWN

< ST AMOS

DAN WADDELL >

WYATT DAVIES >

A

A. THE FRENCH ARE A PASSIONATE PEOPLE UNAFRAID TO SHOOT THEIR MOUTHS OFF AT THE SLIGHTEST PROVOCATION. IN HOSSEGOR, IN SUMMER, THE LIFESAVERS WILL SWIM OUT AND WRESTLE YOU OFF YOUR BOARD IF YOU PERSIST IN SURFING BETWEEN THE FLAGS. HERE, TAJ ARGUES HIS CASE WITH A FRENCH SWIMMER ABOUT WHY HE BELIEVES HE IS JUSTIFIED IN SURFING NEAR NON-SURFERS. THE BODY LANGUAGE OF THE MAN WITH CHAINS SUGGESTS HE FEELS OTHERWISE. B. THE RULES OF THE LINEUP. OBEY THEM, AT LEAST WHEN YOU'RE SURFING WITH YOUR MATES LIKE TAJ HERE IN NORTH-WEST W.A.C. DON'T GET LURED TO THE FRONT SEAT.

RULES OF THE OCEAN

LIKE CALLING WAVE SIZE, THE RULES OF THE OCEAN ARE DIFFICULT TO EXPLAIN TO A BEGINNER. THE RULES ARE BROAD, AND OFTEN VAGUE. SURFING IS BECOMING INCREASINGLY MORE POPULAR. THERE WILL BE TIMES WHEN IT GETS CROWDED AND YOU WILL BE INVOLVED IN A CONFLICT.

Yep, you might be the mellowest person in the world, but it will happen. Don't worry, though. It's cool. It's like any aggro: the outcome simply depends on how you deal with it. I'm not gonna tell you when to shoot your mouth off or let your furious fists fly. I'm just going to explain to you why conflicts happen, and how you can avoid them turning into punch-ups.

YOU, ME, BEACH, NOW...

▶ Fights happen because someone has broken the rules, the main one being the famous drop-in rule. The surfer closest to the breaking part of the wave (the inside) has that wave. Anyone else who takes off on that wave is dropping in. But sometimes it's justified because the surfer on the inside has got there by snaking. If he's jumped off a point or a jetty, or just paddled through the pack straight to the inside, he's a snake, and won't get respect from those who've been waiting their turn. In a pack where people are being nice, the surfer who has been waiting the longest will get the next wave. But that is not going to happen in a beachbreak full of wave pigs. And, on top of all that, you will often encounter locals who think they have priority in any situation. Get the picture? There are no hard and fast rules. Having said that, here's some more pointers:

▶ The person who has waited the longest should get some sympathy, but only if he's trying to maintain his position in the lineup.

▶ Sometimes, the first surfer to paddle for the wave assumes right of way. Not so. Longboarders can sit way further out than anyone, and catch waves more easily. If this rule applied, us short-boarders would get nothing.

▶ If someone snakes you, don't get angry. If you've been snaked and there's another wave behind, not many surfers are going to hassle you for it. Paddle hard, get it, and snap a reo over the snake's head as he's paddling back out. Good surfing is always the best reply.

▶ Be committed. There is nothing more annoying than seeing someone in a good position for a wave pull back. Even if you're gonna cop a beating, take off anyway. Respect, a rare commodity in the lineup, will never come your way if you don't at least have a go.

▶ When someone's surfing toward you, and you're in the way, paddle toward the broken part of the wave.

▶ You may cop the "locals only" crap. Nobody owns the ocean. You have as much right as anyone to be out there. Check page 84 for more of an insight to the localism issue.

▶ Let me explain the top photo here. It's, from left, Crystal Simpson, Dan Waddell, Wyatt Davies, Jay Davies, me, Kerby Brown and Stamos. If this wave was a righthand-breaking point, Stamos would be on the inside, and the next wave would be his. If Kerby is paddling around Stamos to get the inside, he is snaking. By rights, Stamos should have been waiting the longest but this would only happen at a really fair, fantastically democratic break.

If Crystal was sitting out further than everyone and started paddling this right, it wouldn't necessarily be hers. Anyone else could go for it too because she's at the end of the queue.

If this was a left, Crystal would have right of way and Stamos would have the longest to wait for a wave. Jay is sitting out the furthest, but that does not mean he has any more right to any wave, left or right.

The best place to be is in Dan or Wyatt's place. They can catch all the smaller waves without wasting time jockeying for position.

Another waste of time is expecting other surfers to be courteous in the ocean. Do your thing, be true to yourself. Forget how others behave.

TB TIP

BEST SEAT FOR ROAD TRIPS. Forget the front seat, of playing DJ and engaging in idle chit chat with the driver. Let the two talk it up in the front while you drift off to that wonderful little place called sleep in the back seat.

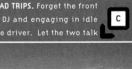

SURFING TINY WAVES

BEFORE WE GET STARTED ON HOW TO SURF TINY WAVES, THERE ARE TWO THINGS YOU SHOULD KNOW: I SOMETIMES HAVE TO FORCE MYSELF TO GO OUT IN TINY WAVES. BUT AFTERWARDS, I'M ALWAYS GLAD I WENT.

Remember that. No matter how cold, small or onshore the surf is, you will always be glad later. The crowd will be relatively small. You will probably get more waves than when it's good, so you'll be free to get a little reckless. Try some new moves, and you might just come in from the session having lifted your surfing up a notch.

SMALL TALK...

▶ I've got a reputation for frothing on small waves at contests. That's because I'm confident I can beat anyone in tiny conditions. It sounds cocky but I know I can nail all of them. On the tour, we pretty much get to say whether we should surf or not. These days, we've got surfers reps who talk to the contest directors. It's weird for me, though, because the moment I even walk up to them when it's small, they just shake their heads, knowing what I'm going to say. "Of course TB wants to surf, he loves it out there."

▶ Surfing small waves is hard work, physically. You struggle to catch them, then struggle all the way to the beach just trying to lay down a couple of moves that look like decent turns. Don't be surprised when you pull off a wave on the shore and realize you're puffing. If nothing else, you're keeping your fitness at its peak.

▶ Board testing. You don't want to waste a session in good waves on a board you're not sure about. The good thing is that small waves are excellent for trying out new shapes. Surfing small waves is hard. If there's something drastically wrong with a board, you'll be able to tell. If I think I've got a good board, I test it out in waves as small as humanly possible.

▶ Speaking of boards, I steer clear of fish and stub boards in tiny waves. It's all 5'11" for this kid. Why? Because to make a board smaller, you've got to add volume in the rail. I'm pretty small so I don't need that (obviously bigger guys do so they can surf in tiny waves).

▶ To make my standard boards go in tiny waves, I've got two secrets. First, only surf tiny waves that are running along a bank. (If it's tiny and dribbling to the beach, you're not going to do much surfing, although the real rank surf works for beginners.) You want to come from behind the peak so you get down-the-line projection. Move your whole stance forward going down the line then shuffle back when you wanna do a turn. Don't make huge direction changes unless you're sure it will bust a big move. On a tiny wave, a big move is likely to be your last, so make sure you've chosen the right spot for it.

▶ Small waves move slowly. When you paddle for them, paddle across at, say, 45 degrees. The wave won't pass you by because it's moving so slowly, and you will take off without wasting any momentum on a bottom turn.

▶ Ride light-footed. Do little floaters and foam climbs. How? Well, that's the second rule: put one foot on the beak! Well, not quite the beak, but really far forward and plough your weight onto that. This keeps momentum.

▶ Once you're in the water, it's often bigger than you thought. And if it isn't you'll struggle on your first waves but adapt as the session progresses. A good example of tiny surf is my section in the new Poor Specimen movie (yep, that's the name). It was at Newport, California. It looked small and crappy, but we hit it anyway. Once I got out there I realised I could get a few good ones. I was just surfing down the line, on the front foot trying to get speed and doing one or two big turns. In tiny waves, quality far exceeds quantity: one good turn is better than three half turns. Use floaters and wash climbs to work up to your big turn.

▶ After successfully surfing tiny waves, the moment you get back on a wave with power, you feel as if you've got the keys to the city. Freedom! No flapping or hopping, just strength in the ocean to move as fast and as loose as you please. That's the main reason you should paddle out when it's hardly breaking: you're in the water, you're surfing. You're losing the jelly legs and you're doing the best training in the world for surfing: surfing!

TB TIP

BODYSURFING IS GOOD FOR YOU. Occasionally leave your board in the car and pop out for a few on your guts. It gets you closer to the wave. You get a feel for the barrel and the contours of the face. And getting pounded is fun.

A

01
03
04

SEQUENCE: SCOTT NEEDHAM/SNPS00C

B

A. TB GETTING CLOSER TO THE WAVES. B. GETTING LOOSE AT TAHITI'S PAPARA BEACH. THERE'S MORE TO TAHITI THAN LEDGING REEFS THAT WANT TO SKIN YOU.

SEQUENCE: RESPONDEK

A

A. FRONTSIDE FLOATERS. HOW GOOD IT FEELS TO STALL OR ACCELERATE OR EVEN SPIN BACKWARDS OFF THE TOP OF A WAVE.   B. AN OLD CANON EOS630. PICK ONE UP CHEAP, GET SOME FRAMES OF YOU AND YOUR BOYS FLARING.

FRONTSIDE FLOATER

THERE ARE TWO REASONS WE DO FLOATERS: TO GET OVER AND AROUND SECTIONS, AND BECAUSE THEY LOOK HOT.

The floater was the first ever surfing trick. Until they came along, moves were all about power. Then the floater showed what could be done using light footwork on a previously unridable part of the wave. You're toying with the wave, daring it to implode and suck you under. Damn, no wonder they look so good.

RUNNING ACROSS THE LIP...

▶ You can float a stinking closeout that's coming towards you, just for the fun of it, or do one to ride over a section you can't get round. The intensity varies according to the wave. Start by floating whitewash, which will forgive your mistakes, then progress to flying over heavy barrel sections, which will punish you severely if you don't know what you're doing.

▶ Don't approach it with a bottom turn, or you'll be committed to a reo instead. You've got to line it up from the start of the previous section. Your feet can be a little further up the board than usual because the aim is travel across the lip for as long as you can. Stay high, do a little pump on the most vertical part of the face and aim your nose straight across the top of the oncoming section, gathering as much speed as you can. If you are approaching the lip late you'll need to throw your arms up as you move up the face so your board and then body get up on the lip as well.

▶ Take the upward thrust of your board in your knees. I mean, bend those things. And add weight to your front foot to conserve speed. Feel the lightness? This is a new kind of move, huh? It's a precarious balance, and as a result you will be tempted to spread your arms out. It's a natural response, but don't do it. Keep them as low as you can. Likewise, you might feel the need to straighten your legs. Don't. You're going to need all your body compression for the hard part, which, believe it or not, you haven't got to yet. Meanwhile, tuck your back knee in and square your shoulders in the direction you're heading.

▶ When you're on the lip, the wave is going to tell you how long you can stay up there. You can get off the wave but it's really tough to hold yourself up there. Two things to know: start coming back down when you feel yourself running out of speed, or the wave is about to cave in. Look at the spot where you want to land, lean your ass out over the drop, twist your body and tweak your ankles to turn your board back towards the beach, and get ready for the fall. Extend your arms to keep yourself centered over the board and extend your legs to take out some of the impact. You need to be light on your feet and drop with weight planted on your back foot or you'll nosedive. Also, there will be water from the breaking lip bouncing back up somewhere near where you want to land your tail. Weight on your back foot will deal with it, and get you ready for a bottom turn on to the next section.

▶ Floaters can nail you with some of your worst small-wave smokings. If the balls of your feet slip off and your board comes up the face between your body and the wave you can get hit in the shins, stomach or face. Yeeeeouch!

TB TIP

SHOOT TO PLEASE. You don't need two grand's worth of gear to take awesome shots of your friends surfing. All you need is a cheap SLR camera and a few rolls of Fuji Reala print film. Get on the net and hunt out a Canon 630 body. It's an old classic and will cost a few hundred bucks. Couple it with a basic telephoto lens (Tamron make a cheapish, but good, 20mm-200mm lens) and you have everything you need for cool wide-angle portraits and for action.

Whack the control dial onto auto (usually a green rectangle), depress the shutter halfway down to activate the autofocus, then fire, fire, fire.

More you shoot, the greater your chance of success.

A. HAPPINESS IS A BACKSIDE FLOATER. YOUR KEY TO MAKING LONG, FOAMY SECTIONS. B. TAJ CHEWS UP A SECTION AT HOME IN WESTERN AUSTRALIA. C. TB AND JAKE PATERSON SHARE A WAVE AT INDONESIA'S VERSION OF DISNEYLAND, THE MENTAWAI ISLANDS.

BACKSIDE FLOATER

THE MOST MEMORABLE SESSION I'VE HAD WITH BACKSIDE FLOATERS WAS RIGHT AFTER *KELLY SLATER IN BLACK AND WHITE* CAME OUT.

I was with my parents at Exmouth, in the north-west of Australia, surfing this really shallow coral reef you can only get to by boat. There were these psycho little lefts and I was just racing down the line, getting up on the lip and hanging there for as long as I wanted then tail-dropping off. It was so sick, landing on almost dry reef, feeling like I was Kelly at Restaurants in Fiji. All I wanted to do was these floats. I was loving it so much it felt like I was never gonna try another turn for the rest of my life. Backside floats are still so fun.

HERE'S THE DEAL...

▶ New backside moves are always daunting because your back's to the wave. Now you're trying to do something that seriously dares the lip to take you out. You don't want to get up there if it's gonna cough you back down, right? Fair bits. That's why you're gonna get on top of that sucker.

▶ You can never be scared of the lip. The moment you're intimidated, you're gonna get smoked. You'll see guys who get up there a little hesitantly and they usually just get horribly smoked, where the board flips under their feet and the fins nail them in the back. When in doubt, do what I did: think you're Kelly at Restaurants.

▶ You don't want to do a stiff bottom turn. Bottom turns are the most important move in surfing, but if you throw down a full-blown bottom turn every time you're at the bottom of a wave, you will butcher a lot of sections. Ease up the face. You know by now what your body must do for this to happen.

Twist out your hips, point your head where you want to go and point your arms at the lip. Sometimes you'll get on the lip too early. This isn't such a big deal. Just hang there. Chances are, if the section looked floatable, it is. It'll fold while you're dancing up there.

▶ Keep your weight centered over your board. If you look at this sequence, you'll notice that in every frame I'm directly over my board.

▶ If the wave's peeling, as opposed to, say, a closeout, you should wait up there until the wave says you've had enough. You'll know this from your forehand floaters. Turn from the lip by putting weight on your front foot and heading toward the beach. Lean into the abyss and twist with your body, keeping your arms down and legs bent to make the drop smoother.

▶ If you hang up there too long, you'll get sucked into the trough and the board will be taken from your feet.

▶ To mix it up and blow people away, when you get on the lip, try to stand tall and really relaxed with your hands by your side.

▶ You can practice floaters on land. Stand in front of a wall about waist high. Jump up on it, using your back foot for most of the jump and bending your knees to make the height. Land on it lightly, then lean back over the edge and get the feel of falling off it. This is so similar to a floater, the way you rise and fall without using much energy. Land with your weight evenly on both feet, and get used to twisting your body into the fall, taking the drop by straightening your legs and balancing

with your arms. Easy, huh? Do it a few times, then paddle out and nail it.

TB TIP

MATE'S RATES. Surfing and learning with a friend is the greatest thing you'll ever do. It'll mean you'll have someone there to drag you out of bed and into a wet wetsuit, it'll mean you've got someone to gauge your own performance against and they'll be your partner in crime when hunting down play with the opposite sex. If you're surfing wedging barrels and they're paddling out, you'll just swing and jump over the falls or something stupid just for fun. You hoot each other into waves, do punts near each other and try to flair so much more because they're paddling back out. You'll do things you'd never do on your own and there's nothing better than that.

A. TAIL HIGH IN A BURNING WESTERN AUSTRALIAN SKY. B. AND IF THERE'S NO PUDDLES, IT'S TIME TO BRING OUT THE SUDS.

HOW TO

FREELOAD WITH STYLE [BY DEREK RIELLY] `PG // 071`

IF YOU SURF YOU WILL TRAVEL, IF YOU TRAVEL YOU WILL WIND UP AT THE MERCY OF OTHERS' HOSPITALITY. HERE'S HOW TO BE A WELCOME FREELOADER...

Nothing gnaws at the soul more than a bitch who milks your hospitality then racks off leaving a smeared toilet, an empty fridge and a nervous dog. Burn one person, one family, and your name in that country is effectively mud. Conversely, a good guest is welcome whenever he's in town and, in time, will be adored as much as any son or daughter. How do you stay on the right side of freeloading law? Follow these tips.

1. Never stay longer than expected. If it could be a week, say so. Don't tell the host you'll be around for two days, then stay fourteen.
2. Get up before the host, clean your space and fold your sleeping gear.
3. Don't stink or be unpleasant to look at. Even if they're not regular habits, wash and deodorise your body and brush your teeth.
4. Only eat what you bring into the house even if the host tells you take what you want.
5. Use the dunny brush to clean your smears in the toilet.
6. Make dinner at least once every week.
7. Insist that you wash up every night.
8. Don't get creepy with the wife or girlfriend of the host. Even dinnertime flirting is enough to get you on the blacklist. Avoid suspicions by never being alone in the house with the wife/girlfriend.
9. Don't throttle bongs or hump chicks.
10. Keep your dirty moods to yourself.
11. Don't change your wax in the lounge room. What's cool in the boy's crib ain't so good when it's in the dream home of your married bud.
12. Don't be painfully polite. Your host shouldn't have to beg you to take a slice of cake.
13. Bring your own towels and keep 'em out of the bathroom when you're not using 'em.
14. In your travels you'll meet men and women who absolutely freak about water on the bathroom floor. As pathetic as it is, keep the peace by mopping all water off the floor with your towel.
15. If you have to abuse the can while the host is in the house, take a box of matches in there with you. One strike and the air is defouled.
16. Get the host up for surfs. If he's a husband and/or a father he'll appreciate the opportunity to leave his homely duties with impunity.
17. The money you find on the floor isn't yours. Hand it over.
18. Don't scare the kids.
19. Stay out of the house during daylight hours. Nothing frustrates a busy family man more than a travelling pal spending long days in front of Judge Mathis and Jerry Springer.
20. Buy 'em a thank-you gift.

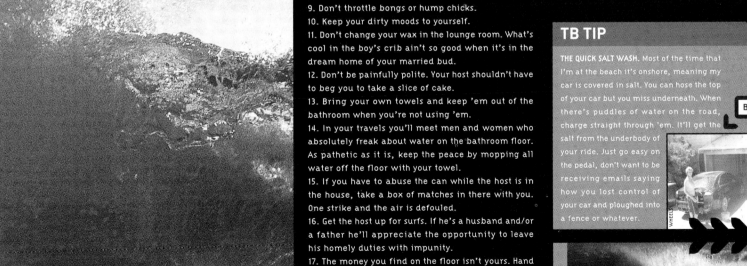

TB TIP

THE QUICK SALT WASH. Most of the time that I'm at the beach it's onshore, meaning my car is covered in salt. You can hose the top of your car but you miss underneath. When there's puddles of water on the road, charge straight through 'em. It'll get the salt from the underbody of your ride. Just go easy on the pedal, don't want to be receiving emails saying how you lost control of your car and ploughed into a fence or whatever.

A

A. YOU'LL NEED THIS TURN. THINK ABOUT IT, PRACTICE IT, DREAM ABOUT IT, PRACTICE IT. B. TB ILLUSTRATES THE POWER OF THE SUN BY TRYING TO STOP THE GAMMAS FROM PHOTOG RESPONDEK'S PRECIOUS FACE.

FRONTSIDE REO

BY DEFINITION, A REO OR RE-ENTRY IS EXACTLY THAT, A TOP TURN THAT RE-ENTERS YOU BACK INTO THE ACTION SO YOU DON'T DROP OVER THE BACK OF THE WAVE.

Twenty years ago a good reo or top turn was pretty spectacular. These days, it's a typical move in any good surfer's quiver. It makes you wonder what's going to be standoid in 20 years time.

Today I was at Caloundra on Queensland's Sunshine Coast for promos and signings. After the promo we bailed to surf at this place called King's Beach. It was two foot and the water was that murky gear water that wrecks your wax. I didn't do much but it was such an eye opener. Andy Irons, Dave Rastovich, Luke Egan, Bede Durbidge, Shaun Cansdell, Wade Goodall and Lawrie Towner were all out there. The performance level was crazy. It was two foot and Wade Goodall was pulling these freaky high punts and supermans. Lawrie Towner was doing these weird barrel rolls on the lefts.

For me, it was the realization of where surfing's headed. Like I've said, surfing should be way more advanced than where it is. But no matter how crazy it gets, frontside reos are an essential move to get wired first.

Reos look best when:
1. You hit it high.
2. The bottom turn is a smooth continuous motion, not a series of mini turns.
3. You hit the lip or wash.
4. You get your board vertical.

How?

▶ To be honest, it's probably easier to do your first serious top turn backside. Okay, I know you've done cutbacks but that's not a reo. Cutbacks are smooth and drawn out. Reos are more of a short, sharp shove.

FROM THE TOP...

▶ Before you can get to the top of the wave, you've first got to come off the bottom. Powerfully. Look at the lip. Or rather, where the lip should be. The secret here is that if you time it right the lip appears when you bottom turn. A good bottom turn is when you keep your drive up the face. A foot toward the tail is essential, as is a decent crouch because you need to extend as you climb the face.

▶ Two options up here. The turn back down. Or the lip bash, which knocks you and your board down back down.

▶ If you get to the top of the wave without a lip it's all about body torque to get you back down. By pointing your arms back to the beach, turning your head to the beach and distributing weight between your feet you'll have successfully done a top turn.

▶ If there's a lip you need to hit the lip with enough weight so you're not knocked off yet with enough grace so it can turn you around and send you back down the face.

▶ Frontside vertical reos are tough. You'll see plenty of photos in surfing magazines of guys sending it north but it takes loads of practice. Your backside lends itself better to reos because it all happens under your body. When you're surfing frontside, it's an extension away from your body.

▶ If you do a reo and get hung up, don't sweat. Just stay with the lip and keep your eye on the bottom of the wave and your arms apart for balance.

▶ Similarly, if you you go for a reo and it turns into a floater then you're

styling. Some of the best turns you ever make are complete mistakes. Try to remember what you did. The wave, the bottom turn, the way it felt. If you can somehow replay it, you've got the gift.

TB TIP

WEAR SUNSCREEN. I don't like wearing zinc (the stuff gets on everything, stinks up your board with dirty marks) but my lips have been so toasted without it. I get really burnt at home because of the ozone hole. I'm the worst little man when it comes to sunscreen. I'm usually frothing over the surf too much to bother. But the sun's power changes everywhere you go. I get less burnt in Hawaii and Europe, yet fried in Indo and Tahiti. It may be overcast but you'll still get burnt. A weathered head, moles and melanomas aren't pretty. Wear the gear.

01

02

04

A

A. THE BACKSIDE RE-ENTRY IS YOUR MOVE FOR COLLECTING ENERGY FROM THE WAVE. EACH TIME YOU HIT THE LIP YOU GATHER MORE SPEED. IT'S A GAMBLE. YOU MIGHT FALL OFF, BUT IF YOU'D RACED AROUND THIS SECTION YOU'D BE FORCED INTO A LIMP CUTBACK TO GET BACK TO THE JUICE. YOU ONLY LIVE ONCE, YOU MAY AS WELL LIVE IT RIGHT. B. IS FOR BOGGED. BUT NOT WITH LOW TIRE PRESSURE.

BACKSIDE REO

I'M NOT A REAL BIG FAN OF THIS SEQUENCE BUT THE ONE BIG PHOTO SHOWS WHAT THE BACKSIDE REO IS ALL ABOUT: BODY TORQUE AIMED AT THE LIP. I THINK ABOUT BACKSIDE REOS ALL THE TIME BECAUSE THERE ARE SO MANY TYPES AND STYLES.

You can smash it vertically, approach it upside-down or throw your tail (see page 106). I love doing backside reos at Macaronis in Indo. It's such a perfect peeling wave you can smash one and then there's another section waiting. The best thing is each turn gives you confidence to do a bigger turn next time. By the end of the wave, because it peels so perfectly, you're throwing down these huge snaps, pushing each turn a little bit more than the one before.

TORQUE IT UP...

▶ If you do a backside reo like this too early, you won't get up the section. Do it too late and your board will go over the back and you'll fall flat on your face. You need to pick your section, be confident and deal with that lip.

▶ First, never be frightened of the lip. The moment you go soft will be the moment you get licked. Confidence is the key.

▶ If there's a section above you, hit it. Your arms and eyes are most important here. Notice in the first frame I'm looking straight up at the lip. This is important in nailing the turn.

▶ Twist your body. Notice that my body torque through the sequence is what pulls me toward the lip. Pull your front arm and hand behind your head. This will pull you up the face.

▶ Keep your eyes on the lip as you move up the face, pushing with your back foot on your heel as you bottom turn. Keep the weight there as you move toward the lip. If you're just starting these moves, skip the next two tips.

▶ From here, you can really mix it up. If you keep some weight on your front foot, you can push some more on your back foot and flare the tail over the lip. It is a sliding transition of the turn, so you'll often push too hard and slide too much. It's tough to recover from here because your heelside rail will bog and you'll spin out.

▶ The speed of the turn depends on how intense the lip is. If you're just hitting foam, the move can be as slow and mellow as you like. But if you're hitting a lip, be prepared for a sudden change of direction, a lot of power being forced into your legs and a full 180-degree turn. Never come down sideways in front of the lip. It'll take you out. Instead, go with it, and use it.

▶ So now you wanna get back down. Look where you want to go. Don't let doubt creep into your mind – stay centered over your board. If you've lost a lot of speed and you find yourself on the face with your board facing straight down, you're going to nosedive. There's not much you can do about this, except maybe learn from your mistake. Like most moves, there is a fine line between pushing it to the limit and washing off so much momentum that you're powerless to recover.

TB TIP

DRIVING YOUR CAR ON SAND.
It's good idea to let your tires down as low as possible. I let mine down a little bit so I can drive on the beach and on the main roads. If you're really stuck in the sand, let 'em down real low, and getting out will be easier.

PHOTOS: RESPONDEK

A. UP, ACROSS, BACK DOWN, AWAY. FOAM CLIMBS ARE YOUR BEST MATE WHEN IT'S ONSHORE OR SECTIONY. B. WHEN'S YOUR BOARD NOT GOING FLING BACK IN YOUR FACE? WHEN YOU KICK OUT OF A WAVE WITH IT GLUED TO YOUR FEET.

FOAM CLIMBS

WE'VE ALL GOT DIFFERENT COMFORT ZONES. I TRIED TO GO TO THE BIG DAY OUT IN PERTH LAST YEAR AND IT SERIOUSLY RATTLED ME. IT'S KINDA WEIRD BECAUSE I'VE BEEN SEMI-MOBBED IN PLACES LIKE BRAZIL BUT THIS OCCASION KINDA FREAKED ME. I WAS CRUISING WITH FRIENDS AND WE WERE JUST GOING TO HAVE A NORMAL DAY CHECKING OUT BANDS AND WHATEVER BUT THEN I NOTICED HEAPS OF PEOPLE WERE LOOKING AT ME.

02

03

04

It was like the worst ever case of having food in my teeth and everyone knew except me. Actually it was more like I was walking around with my prong hanging out of my fly. It was heavy. The reason I'm off riding crazy tangents is because we've all got levels of discomfort. For a lot of people I know, foam climbs freak them out. They're not the most flashy turn. You usually just do them while you're waiting for the wave to really fire up. I like to bust them in a few scenarios, mostly as a reo using the foam as an oversized lip to get to the clear face; but also as a post-closeout play thing. When a wave's shut down and you've still got speed to burn, a foam climb's a hot ticket to fun.

Thing is, you're playing with foam. Foam's unpredictable and gives you those embarrassing slow-motion wipe-outs when you know you're falling and the wave's going to peel off without you on it. Once that happens, there's nothing you can do about it.

EACH WAY, EVERY DAY...

▶ Backside or frontside, the same principles apply to wash climbs. The most important thing to remember is to be committed and confident. Don't be timid or you'll catch an edge and cop the slow-mo frustrating fall.

▶ More than any other turn, the wash climb is about your arms. They don't get in the water but they are instrumental in shifting your body up off the face and onto the foam.

▶ Couple the arm movement with a good bottom turn and you'll be riding high on the powdery gear. You gotta hit that foam with a trajectory or you're finished, okay? Don't ride it flat.

▶ It's real tough to be beside the wash, kick up your inside rail and climb to victory. This is only possible when you're going really fast but unless you've got incredible control your board tends to shoot up the face and you fall forward.

▶ If you try from right beside the wash without speed your board will be caught by the foam and it'll just get kicked back down. You need to be moving on your trajectory as you approach the wash. Almost vertical's the go.

▶ So it's a short, sharp bottom turn and a swift movement of your arms toward the top of the wave. They'll feel strange but you seriously have to throw your arms up. You'll be amazed at how effective your arms are. Like most turns when you get on the lip, all you've got to do is look back down the wave and you're clear.

TB TIP

PULL THE OTHER ONE. You've wiped out or bailed, come up behind the wave and can feel the pull on your leash. Cool, you think, my board will be coming back any second now. Well, it might be coming back sooner, and faster, than you think. That leash can fling your board at you at a frightening speed. And what's floating just above your surface, where your board is headed? That's right. Your face. Hold a hand up to protect you, but be prepared to duck under if it's coming back too fast. As a rule, the longer you wait for the board to come out of the whitewater, the faster it's gonna come shooting out. Don't let it hit you.

TWIGGY

A & B. TB TRAVELS NINE MONTHS OF THE YEAR, USUALLY WITH A DOZEN BOARDS AND ARMED WITH ENOUGH GEAR TO PROVIDE A LITTLE PIECE OF HOME ON THE ROAD. EVEN WHEN YOU'RE A TOP PROFESSIONAL SURFER THERE'S MOMENTS OF LONELINESS WHEN A FAMILIAR BOOK OR CD WILL TAKE THE STING OUT. C. KEEP YOUR EYE ON DINGS AND ESPECIALLY WATCH THOSE CHEEKY TAIL/RAIL DINGS. GRIEF!

PACKING YOUR BOARDS

I WAS IN CALIFORNIA ON SEPTEMBER 11. I WALKED OUT OF MY HOTEL TO GO TO AN EXPRESSION SESSION AND THERE WERE A FEW PEOPLE GATHERED AROUND TVs, WATCHING SOMETHING. I WASN'T SURE WHAT WAS GOING ON. THEN I GOT PICKED UP AND DIDN'T TAKE TOO MUCH NOTICE.

When I got to the beach, everyone was freaking out, and I realized what had actually gone down. Five days later I'm at LA airport and the queue goes from inside to about a hundred yards down the footpath. I kiss my Qantas platinum frequent flyers' card and go straight to the front to get out of there. A year later, the bombs in Bali bring this horror show way closer to home. But I'm not gonna analyze it because I'm sure you've heard enough about it already.

So we live in a different world. Am I gonna change? Nup. Should you? That's your choice. But let me tell you this: as a surfer, you need to travel. You need to pull up and see that Off the Wall, Backdoor and Pipe are all basically one peak. You need to struggle with languages, surf on beaches with black sand, take in different cultures. The more places your surf, the more you'll realize just how many perfect waves there are in the world.

In my early days of traveling I used to total lots of boards. Lately, though, they almost always arrive at the other end in perfect nick. I recently flew home from Brazil with one too many boards in my bag. It only just squeezed in. I knew it was a risk, but I went with it anyway. No protective fin blocks, no nuthin. The bag came through the oversized baggage door at Perth airport with a set of fins sitting perfectly through the boardbag. They'd driven through but other than that everything in the coffin was sweet.

You sign board-damage waivers for your boards when you travel so you've got to take good care of 'em.

KEEPING YOUR BOYS SAFE...

▶ The size of your board bag depends on the number of boards you're taking. You're investing money to score waves, so please take more than one board. It doesn't matter how good or bad you surf, or how careful you are, you board can always be snapped or stolen.

▶ A few rules when you're packing a few boards: the board on the bottom should be laid deck down. And that's the way it's gotta stay for every board on top. Start mixing rockers on top of each other and you'll be opening a very ugly boardbag when you arrive.

▶ Some boardbags have plastic dividers to put between your boards; no big deal if they don't but if they're there, use 'em. If not, lay a wettie or towel between them, this'll stop you getting wax on the bottom of your boards. The way to sort is nose to tail, the nose sitting between the fins of the board below. Be careful to always put padding under the nose (a towel or vest'll do) or you'll wind up with dents down there. If you stack them up all the same end, you'll fit less in and have more chance of snapping out fins.

▶ Packing boards is a piece of cake with detachable fins. But I have fixed fins 'cause I like my boards to feel tight, solid and drivey. So, when packing, I use fin guards. They're the best thing ever invented. Check the first photo in the sequence. They protect the fins, you don't get wax on the bottom of your board, and the whole tail is protected. They used to take up more room but I've recently customized them by cutting out the center (see photos). Otherwise, use towels or wetties. Gotta save those fins.

▶ Some people pile their clothes in their boardbags but I reckon you should keep it light. You're allowed two bags at check-in and if your board bag is reasonably light, it's way easier not to get stung for excess baggage.

▶ Travel costs. But good waves on a good board with you in good form is priceless. Enjoy your money, get memories with it. Money is there to be spent. Only thing worth buying is fun, afterall.

TB TIP

HOW SOLAREZ CAN SAVE YOUR LIFE. Premixed resin that dries in five minutes in the sun is perfect for sealing those rail dings that could lead to snaps or a brown board. Don't be lazy. Seal that baby and get more value from your board.

globe

A

A. SOMETIMES WHEN YOU'RE SURFING A HEAVY REEF IT'S BETTER NOT TO KNOW WHAT'S ON THE BOTTOM. A FISH EYE VIEW OF BACKDOOR. B. ON RAIL AT A WAKEBOARDING SESSION IN VICTORIA WITH TONY HAWK.

COOL STORY

[NORTH POINT BITES] PG // 081

TB'S HEAD MEETS THE NORTH POINT REEF. HERE'S A BLOW-BY-BLOW ACCOUNT OF WHAT WENT DOWN...

Saturday May 25, 2002.

5.30am. It's dark when I wake up and I know the swell's big and offshore. It's strange but you just know: the wind's warm, the air's moist and you can almost feel the wave movement in the air. A quick coffee and piece of toast to clear the sleep from the eyes and I'm on.

5.50am. Pack the wagon with three sticks – a 6'1", 6'4" and a 6'6" – and I'm off to North Point.

6.20am. The surf's good but whoa, it's crowded. Two contests are in town and there's gotta be 30 guys in the water already. I don't care though, North Point doesn't break much and I'm away most of the year. There's no way in the world I'm not going out. Eight foot and offshore, there's no decision.

6.35am. I'm waxed up, done a 10 second stretch (I don't really believe in stretching) and make my way down to the rocks. I jump off the side of the rocks - not out around the back or through the bay – 'cause I need to get out there as quickly as possible.

8.15am. Break a craft as I kick out through the back of a closeout. There goes the 6'4". I grab my 6'6". It's a dodgy craft and doesn't hold in that well. That's all you need a board to do at North Point: hold its line in the face.

9.45am. A good one comes through, about an eight footer. As I'm paddling into it I get the feeling you get when you know you're into a bomb. I take off and pull up into a big, big cave. I know I'm deep but I'm thinking I'll be able to drive through it. I do a speed pump or two and think I'm going to be alright when the shockwave just hits me and takes me out. My board gets sucked from under me and then I'm slammed headfirst into the reef. The strangest thing is I'm way out the back where it's typically deep. At North Point, the only place you hit the bottom is on the inside. It doesn't even feel that powerful a wipeout. As soon as I penetrated the water I must've just been pole-driven headfirst straight down into the reef. I didn't even realise I was upside down when my head just slammed into the reef. Two years earlier I'd pulled out Grant Boxall as a paraplegic (see page 120) from the same injury. Heavy.

So am I gone? Is my neck toast? Do I care?

Nup. I don't care how long I'm under for, I'm just dazed waiting to get to the top. I put my hands out ahead of me like I'm touching the ceiling to get out of there.

9.46am. Once I reach the surface, the rattle hits for real. I feel like a wreck, messed up. I grab my neck, everything seems pretty cool. I put my hand on my head and when I look at it again, it's covered in red. I get washed in, crawl up the rocks and start losing my balance a bit. Then a bodyboarder comes up and checks it out. "Ah, it's not... that... bad but you'll need stitches," he says kinda reluctantly. It doesn't rattle me too much... and then I see another guy. He's like, "Mate, I can see your skull!"

9.50am. ASP judge Perry Hatchett is on the rocks and throws me in his truck. We bolt to Margaret River hospital.

10.30am. Turns out there are two holes. The needles are driven into my skull and the first hole takes nine staples to close, the second three. The last staple is inserted out of the anesthetised area and the pain is incredible. As I'm leaving, a bodyboarder comes in with blood pouring from his head.

Good ol' North point, always the master.

TB TIP

GET YOUR SURFING THRILLS WHENEVER, HOW-EVER YOU CAN. People who say they surf every day are liars. It is not physically possible to surf every day of the year. Everywhere gets flat. Still, that doesn't mean you can't get your surfing thrills elsewhere. It's all balance, it's all practise, it's all fun.

WIPING OUT THE RIGHT WAY

CALL IT WHAT YOU LIKE - GETTING SMOKED, LICKED, TOASTED OR SMASHED. IT'S GOING TO HAPPEN. SO IF YOU DON'T LIKE IT, TAKE THE WAX OFF YOUR BOARD, SLIDE IT INTO YOUR BOARDBAG AND GET IT TO THE PAWNBROKERS.

If you're still with me, here's some more gory grits. There'll be times when you think you're going to die – seriously – and other times when you'll be underwater and you won't know which way is up. I've had staples driven into my scalp after a wipeout at North Point, been stretchered off the beach after bouncing off the reef during the Pipe Masters and I've pulled a semi-unconscious guy from the water after he hit the reef near my house. So I'm not going to sit here and tell you that you won't get hurt. But I will share a few thoughts on how to get licked in the safest way possible.

▶ Straight up, don't go trying any of that macho run-into-the-shorey-and-somersault stuff. That's a one-way express ticket to wheelchairville. Sand banks always change. Leave the tricky gear to the geese in the Olympics.

▶ When you're learning, the chance of a serious wipeout is pretty rare. You'd have to lunge headfirst into rocks or something, or get driven through your board by a double-overhead lip. As a learner, I reckon you'll be steering clear of this kinda stuff.

▶ Try not to surf solo, especially at rock-bottoms or reefs. Hit your head and knock yourself out, you're finished.

▶ Never lunge yourself forward when aborting your ride. Jump to the side, drop over the back, just make sure your feet and body hit the water before your shoulders, neck and head. Do what I say, don't do what I do. I hate the photo on this page. It really freaks me. It's a habit I'm losing.

SAND AIN'T ALWAYS SOFT...

▶ Just because we're talking sand, doesn't mean it's cute and yellow and soft. It packs like concrete down there and can do some damage. There's the risk of spinal injury. If you fall headfirst into the sand, you could be in some real trouble. Likewise, you can fall heavily and still surface fine. It's the unpredictability of playing in mother nature's kitchen.

▶ The best thing about getting licked on a beachbreak is you've always got a surface to push from. Unlike reef, which cuts your feet, you've got a sand platform to get you to safety. If your leggie isn't pulling tight with pressure, make sure you surface with your hands above your head. When your lungs are out of air the last thing you want is face full of fins.

The Reef Police...

▶ If you even touch the bottom at some joints, you're gonna get cut up. Places like Bingin in Bali look so playful and fun and groovy but when you hit the reef, you know about it.

▶ If you're surfing some super shallow ledge don't wear a leggie that's too long. If it gets snagged on the reef, you can be dragged underwater. And to get real grim, maybe... uh... drown.

▶ Booties protect your feet but feel weird. Difficult to surf in at the start, after a while they feel really grippy. The worst thing is, when you go back to surfing with your bare hooves, it's as if your board's been soaped. And they look pretty crook. Good at G-land and Ulus but the fashion ball's in your court here, kids.

▶ Generally, the smaller the surf is, the shallower the water over reef. Don't be fooled, small days are when you're gonna be ripped apart.

▶ When you're paddling out and the water is drawing off the reef, lay shallow in the water. This way your fins won't get ripped to shreds.

▶ Starfish (lay spreadeagled) when you wipe out. You don't want to thrash around and get your legs hacked up on the reef.

On Rock...

▶ Surfing over rock bottoms is similar to reefs because you have to worry about the severe danger of smashing into it and getting KO'd. The good thing is most of the time you can use it to push yourself from if you're under there getting roughed up.

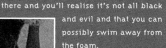

TB TIP

THE GOLDEN RULES OF WIPEOUTS

▶ Never fall headfirst.

▶ Never fight too much underwater.

▶ Chill, your lungs really aren't that small.

▶ If you're in clear water, don't be afraid to open your eyes. It lessens the fear down there and you'll realise it's not all black and evil and that you can possibly swim away from the foam.

▶ Never give up. Wait for the ocean to say it's all over, not the word from upstairs. Think about it, the best tube, the best air, the best turns you've ever done, you wouldn't have expected to make.

A

I hate this photo. I have a bad habit of diving head first,
and the consequences scare me!
this is not wiping out the right way thats for sure!

should be
here →

my home break and i
still cant make the drop.

X
ridiculously shallow sand here

↑ turn page to check awkward body position
and rank head shot.

I hate this photo. I have a bad habit of diving head first, and the consequences scare me. this is not wiping out the right way thats for sure!

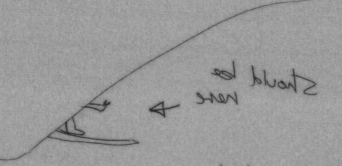

Should be here →

my knee broke and i still can't make the drop.

X
ridiculously Shallow Sand here

t b's
BOOK OF HOT SURFING

SEQUENCE: TWIGGY

B

A. A CLOSE-UP OF TAJ'S HEAD PRIOR TO SPECTACULAR IMPACT. B. HOW DO YOU WIPE OUT? DEFINITELY NOT HEAD FIRST. THIS IS TAJ BREAKING EVERY RULE IN HIS OWN BOOK.

TIM JONES

A

A. NORTH POINT, ONE OF TB'S FAVOURITE WAVES, AS LONG AS IT'S NOT BOUNCING HIM ON THE SHELF AND SENDING HIM TO HOSPITAL TO HAVE STAPLES PUT IN HIS SKULL. (SEE THE PREVIOUS SPREAD FOR THAT PARTICULARLY BLOODY STORY.) B. KEEP THE SAND OFF THE DECK BY STABBING YOUR CRAFT INTO THE SAND.

WHY LOCALS
DESERVE RESPECT

I'VE BEEN THINKING ABOUT THIS ONE A LOT LATELY. I WAS SURFING AT INDJINUP, AND THE WAVES WERE REALLY FUN. WHEN I PADDLED OUT, EVERYONE RECOGNISED ME, AND CONGRATULATED ME FOR WINNING A RECENT EVENT IN BRAZIL. IT WAS COOL, BUT BENEATH ALL THE GOODWILL LURKED SOMETHING POTENTIALLY UGLY.

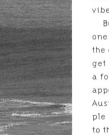

The guys in the line up were letting me have every wave I paddled for. I could've caught every wave out there if I wanted. And that was the moral dilemma I was in. I could've done it all day and they would've gone in thinking I was a spoilt little prick, even though they were letting me do it! I had to chill. So every time I paddled out after a wave, I paddled past the pack, right out the back. Whenever a set came, I let everyone else get one before I took off. I felt really good afterward. Everyone respected each other, and the vibe was happy.

But there are no specific rules. Everyone who starts surfing is thrown in at the deep end. We all know surfing can get nasty. Our cover was blown when a former world champion, Nat Young, appeared in Sunday newspapers across Australia with a smashed face. People who didn't surf quickly likened it to the anger drivers get when they find themselves sharing crowded roads, and called it surf rage. But anyone who surfs knows it goes deeper than that.

Each break has its dominant surfers who surf it whenever it's on - whether it's pumping, stormy onshore or one-foot mush. The older they are, the more respect they think they deserve.

I know it's a free world and nobody owns the ocean and everyone should have equal rights to whatever break they like but... it's the way it is. Almost every break in the world has locals. Even at breaks without them you will find someone at least trying to claim the title. Some are nothing more than loud-mouthed gibbons sitting out the back, yelling "fuggoff touros" and "locals only". Others, though, can be patient, silent assassins who wait until you torment them one too many times, then send you to the beach to sort it out in the traditional, stupid manner. Why? Because, as mad as it sounds, we're humans. We're passionate! We love what we do and love where we do it. We're alpha males. Strangers are a threat. We want what's ours!

If you surf, you will experience localism, though it will come in different packages. There's the face-to-face or fist-to-face dealing as above. You can be sent in. Your car can be trashed – its tires slashed, windows waxed, or the whole thing burnt to the ground. If you're surfing a break that has a history of this type of localism, park where you can see your car from the water (and make sure you've got comprehensive insurance!)

Plenty of locals are like seagulls – hovering about making lots of noise, and quick to fly off when challenged. Not that standing up to angry locals is what it's about. I rarely get into conflict in the water. That's because I'm a frother. I'm out there to catch as many waves as possible, which usually means picking up the smaller ones that nobody else wants. It's the easiest way to get waves in any line-up. Flare on them and the locals will be more likely to give you a look in when the sets come.

Localism only starts when people who surf a place all the time feel threatened by encroaching crowds. Surfing is becoming more popular, and localism will only get worse. There is no use getting worked up about it.

You've got two options. One, surf the world, picking up the scraps when there are locals about and gorging yourself when there aren't. Or, two, become a local at your break. Surf it constantly. For every 30 average surfs you have, you'll feel as if you own it on those rare perfect days.

TB TIP

STORING YOUR BOARD ON THE BEACH. Sand on your wax and over your wettie isn't cool. Drive the nose of your board into the sand at about a 45 to 60 degree angle with the bottom up and you're styling: plus you can use your fins to hold your wettie and towel. Make sure there are no rocks underneath and don't push it in so hard that you break it.

A

A. THE VARIOUS METHODS OF STOWING A SURFBOARD. GOOD GOD ALMIGHTY, IT'S ALL SO EASY! B. CHECK THE EFFORT IN THIS PUNT, GETTING LUKE EGAN'S 6'4" TANK OUT OF THE WATER ON AN EAST COAST ROAD TRIP.

GETTING 'ROUND

WITH YOUR CRAFT

A CAR IS FREEDOM. I WENT FOR MY DRIVING TEST THE MOMENT I TURNED 17. I FAILED, AND I WAS SO DEVASTATED. I FOUND OUT LATER THAT THE GUY WHO DID THE TEST PERFORMED THE SAME TRICK ON EVERYONE.

I'd been driving really well. Then he took me down this really long dirt road. I had the most intense concentration. So we were in the middle of nowhere on a dead-end road. Casually, he said: "Throw a U-turn down here." So I did the u-bolt and drove back to the registry. We got out and he said, you didn't indicate when you did that u-turn. YOU FAIL. Indicate! On a deserted dirt track! I was so rattled.

The first thing I asked was when I could go again. I went back the next week, used my indicator and within minutes had a laminated license with this crazy big smile on it. I swear, it was the most amazing thing ever. And my parents were more stoked than me. Taking me surfing every day after school for all those years ended right then and there.

There isn't a car that exists that isn't capable of carrying you and your craft to the beach. It may not always be legal, it may not always be comfortable. But if it works, it'll do.

SO YOU BOUGHT A CAR, EH KID?

Here's how you're gonna get your boards in it or on it.

▶ If it's a sedan that doesn't have a fold-down back seat, the front-seat trick is the easiest. All you do is fold back your front passenger seat, feed the nose of the board through the door over the driver's side seat and lay it flat in the passenger seat. And depending on your car, you can pile a few in here. Wrap the seatbelt around them so they don't swing around when you belt round corners. Turns out to be a bit tight if you've three mates in the back but crank up the back speakers and they'll be right.

No roof racks?

▶ Not such a big deal. Racks are for when you've got a few boards or boardbags. Other than that, they're not essential. Without boardbags, roll two towels to create a set of roof racks. Lay your boards on top (tails to the front) and thread tie downs through the car. Make sure the doors are open so the tie downs don't go through the windows. Otherwise, you'll have to climb out the window *Dukes of Hazzard*-style. Also, if it rains it's all over. You're gonna get wet because the rain runs down the straps and drips into the car. It really is grief.

Do leashes work?

▶ They're a bit dodgy if you don't have roof racks because you have to close the car door on them. Leashes are the quickest and easiest if you have one board on roof racks. All you do is put your board tail first, leave your leash attached to the car and wrap it around the tail and leave the nose sitting there free if you're only going to be cruising around town.

▶ To stop tie downs buzzing, twist up the cord after they're secure.

Illegal options

▶ I've seen guys holding boards out of windows like they were riding a pushie. Pretty easy to get caught by the wind and whipped out of your hand.

▶ You can poke the nose out of the window but get the wrong cop and you're finished.

▶ Other tips: Pull straps firm but not too tight, or you'll chew through the rails. Use board bags when you can. Remember, wax is gonna get on everything, so lay towels between. The top board should have a board bag or it'll get toasted brown by the sun. Don't use Occy tie-downs. Oh, and if you wanna look pro, pack your boards inside, not on top. Your boards will move around on racks. But that doesn't necessarily mean they're destined to ride under the wheels of the semi behind you. And one more thing: if you surf a lot, at some point your boards will come off the roof. It's character building.

TB TIP

FROM BIG BOARDS TO SMALL. Not loving your shortboard? Sick of bogging rails or just can't make it flare any more? Jump on the biggest, ugliest board you can find. Do 20 minutes, do two hours. Chances are the next sesh on your old board will be fast and free. It'll feel like an extension of your limbs. Seriously.

A. TB IN HIS *MAD MAX* KIT. READERS MIGHT LIKE TO LEARN THAT MR SHERMAN NAMED HIS FIRST-BORN CHILD TAJ, AFTER HIS FAVORITE SUBJECT.
B. EVEN IN THE MIDDLE OF THE INDIAN OCEAN, YOU CAN REMEMBER BIRTHDAYS. TEEBS AND HIS SWEET TWENTY-SECOND IN SUMATRA.

HOW TO

BREAK AMERICA THE ROCKSTAR WAY [BY DEREK RIELLY] PG // 089

PHOTOGRAPHER STEVE SHERMAN INTRODUCES TAJ TO THE US WITH HIS CLASSIC MAD MAX PORTRAITS...

Wasn't that long ago that TB was an unknown outside of Australia, his natural talent only a rumor to surfers abroad. The child of American parents, and a mad fan of the *Momentum* crew, it's rad how long it took for the US to dig on the kid's act.

California based magazine *Transworld Surf*, the world leader in lifestyle surf photography thanks to staff shooter Steve Sherman, decided to break TB in the States with a major profile and a conceptual portrait shoot.

"*Mad Max* is a favorite movie of mine," says Steve Sherman. "It's the whole Mel Gibson thing. It's essentially Australian and it made sense – in a weird sorta way – to get Taj in *Mad Max* gear."

Sherm and *TWS* editor Chris Cote rented *Mad Max* and spent hours carefully studying the movie to make sure TB's outfit was authentic. Chris wound up buying an old football shoulder pad set from a garage sale and Sherm cut up a 15-year-old black leather jacket from his punk days (a sleeve was ripped off to mimic the movie's hero). Add goggles, a bandage, attitude and you have the Taj Burrow as *Mad Max* experience.

Sherm flew to Hawaii specifically to do the photos, hooked up with Taj who was staying in a North Shore pad, grabbed a garbage bin and filled it with dirt and drove the ensemble to a junkyard on the Eastside near Goat Island. Sherm, Taj and local surfer Pete Johnson who brought his dog for the photos of Taj walking down a lonesome road, jumped the fence and set up the lights.

Taj climbed into his gear. Sherm grabbed handfuls of dirt and rubbed it into Taj's face. All were constantly looking over their shoulders 'cause the Eastside is the sorta joint you don't want to be busted trespassing in some lunatic's wrecking depot. Sherm shot five rolls of Taj on his old Mamiya box camera and ran off a roll on his standoid 35mm Nikon in case the box stuff didn't work (it did).

Says Taj: "I freaked and was gonna ask him if we could bar it and shoot something more mellow. But, of course, he insisted saying, '*Mad Max* is rad, man! This is gonna look so cool!' There was no way I could shut down a kid with this much froth so the skinny boy jumped into the big man's outfit, wrapped bandages around my arm, rubbed dirt on my face and started nailing the shots. When I saw the results I was stoked!"

When the April 2000 issue went on the stands and the feature Taj Burrow – the Road Warrior filtered into the surfing world's consciousness, the response was... loud.

"Billabong's Marketing Director in the USA, Graham Stapleberg, freaked out!" says Sherm. "Said it was the best way for Taj to be introduced to the US. Everyone loved it. Some people thought it was the best thing we'd done at *Transworld*. It was *so* Australian. It hit the nail on the head."

TB TIP

FRIENDS LOOK AFTER FRIENDS.
Milestones are cool. Birthdays are cool. Good friends who go out of their way for their mates are cool. If it's a birthday and there's nothing planned, hook a brother up with a cake or a case of beer. Yeah, most kids play down the day but we all enjoy being thought of.

SOMETIMES YOU JUST GOTTA BREATHE. SOMETIMES IT'S ALL SCHOOL, WORK, PARENTS, GIRLS, WHATEVER, AND THE ONLY THING THAT'S GOING TO REFIRE THE PISTONS IS TO ALIGN YOUR RAIL INTO A FAVORITE WAVE. THIS IS TAJ'S. THIS IS HIS RELEASE.

A

POWER, PRECISION, POISE. ENOUGH PRACTICE AND YOU'LL BURY YOUR RAILS DEEP AND STRONG LIKE TEEBS HERE.

THROWING HEAT

It's not about hours in the ocean, number of weeks you've been surfing or how old you are. This section chooses you, you don't choose it. How do you know you're ready for this section? Where are you in the big picture of surfing talent? Here's a bit of a guide... You see boats in a harbor and straight away know what the wind is doing. You fix your owns dings, the day you get them. You notice the surf in the background of a clichéd car ad when the convertible speeds round cliff-top roads. Wet wetsuits don't scare you. You get excited when you see an intense low on a weather map. You watch a wipeout and accurately predict a broken board You flick through surf mags and almost always know where the shot was taken, even though there's no land as an indicator in the photo.

This section's all about refinement. How to hit the wash higher on roundhouse cutbacks, grabbing a rail in tight spots and getting your top turns actually to the top. If you're here, you already know a lot about surfing so I won't be too specific. Don't wanna flood you with the gear you already know, okay? Let's ride...

03

02

04

A

A. THE PERFECT FRONTSIDE ROUNDHOUSE – FLUID, POWERFUL, ACCURATE, STYLISH. AN ESSENTIAL PART OF EVERY SURFER'S REPERTOIRE. B. WHAT'S HIP? ACCA DACCA AND THE FIN THROW.

ROUNDHOUSE CUTBACK

EVER SEEN A POINTBREAK SURFER WHO CAN'T DO CUTBACKS? I LOVE AIRS, BUT A MAN IN GOOD SURF WHO CAN'T WET HIS RAILS AIN'T PRETTY.

Cutbacks and roundhouse cutbacks, is there a difference? You know there is. A roundhouse cutback is where you do a cutback and follow it through with a backside reo off the wash. You can do a cutback with a little slide at the end and the wash can hit you on the back but until you're actually turning off the wash, doing a full figure eight, it's not a roundhouse.

BACK TO THE SOURCE...

▶ To start to get the feel for doing the whole turn, you should concentrate on getting your board all the way round. My big rule is where you look is where you go. The same with your arms, where they point is where they'll send your body.

▶ There are plenty of good sections to do roundhouse cutbacks. If you're racing toward a closeout that looks too dangerous to smack, turn around and do a roundhouse instead. Where you've been, which is the spot you will hit, will always be less nasty then where you're headed. And it sure beats pulling off the wave and wasting all that precious speed.

▶ Fat waves. If you've reached the end of a wave and there's no wall to do a turn, a roundhouse is a good – and pretty much your only – option. Here it's going to be more difficult to smack the wash, you'll just do a little foam climb. Still fun, though.

▶ Another good one is straight from the take-off. Rather than dropping down and trying a reo straight away, race away from the peak and lay over a big roundhouse cuttie. Sometimes I'm so psyched to get all air crazy and

race to a section but it feels good to slow it down and throw a big roundie.

▶ So, getting that thing nailed. When you're getting started, don't do too big a bottom turn or you'll lose all your speed which you need to cover some serious ground. Race away from the wash and do a slower style bottom turn up the face. You're turning off your inside rail so your back foot will need to be right on the tail.

▶ When you get to the top of the wall, don't jam hard on your tail. It is tempting, I know, but don't. Instead, you wanna do a drawn-out arc, keeping your body relatively constant throughout it. If you look at the bottom of the wave and keep your weight fairly even, you'll get the first bit of the arc done fairly well. Add a little back foot pressure if you feel you're not getting round quick enough or you're gonna nosedive.

▶ Once the wash is within your range of vision (without twisting your neck too much), look at it. That's what you're gonna hit. Move your arms towards it. Keep your weight even, and prepare for the rebound. Don't let it freak you out. It's fun, and it's not even slightly dangerous. Blowing it is not gonna hurt you. You'll always think you've left the rebound part too late and won't be able to get up there. You can. Ignore the feeling your foot's on the tail, your eyes are telling you where you're headed, you'll be sweet. Just throw your arms a touch more vertically and your board will follow.

▶ When you feel your board hit the wash, you already need to be looking

at the bottom of the wave because this is now where you want to be. By looking down, your board will twist and it will be as if you've done a backside reo. Put weight on your front foot as this will help you ride over the wash to the bottom of the wave.

▶ In the early days, don't bother trying to smack a reo, just get the motion down. Just by tapping the wash, it'll look like a reo.

▶ At the start, you'll probably run out of steam before you reach the wash. You may hit the wash but have no speed to get back down the wave. Keep it slow at the start, get the motion down and then start trying reos.

TB TIP

TO A TEE. An old T-shirt you'd never wear on the street again is the perfect summer surfing accessory. Imperfections and rips add to the effect. Chicks dig tees, it does the same job as a rash shirt without the 30-skins cost and doesn't inhibit your surfing. Way cooler than a skin-tight rashie.

B

SEQUENCE: TWIGGY

A

A. BACKHAND CUTBACKS ARE PROBABLY THE FIRST REAL MOVE YOU'LL MASTER. PERFECT YOUR FRONTSIDE BOTTOM TURN, START IT AT THE TOP OF A B/S WAVE FACE, AND YOU'VE GOT YOURSELF A DATE WITH SURFING DESTINY. B. WHOA, WHOA, WHOA! GO EASY. A COUPLE OF PILLS ONLY NOT A MEDICINE CABINET.

ROUNDHOUSE CUTBACK

THIS SHOT WAS TAKEN AT MACARONIS IN INDONESIA. YOU HAVE NO IDEA HOW PERFECT THIS WAVE IS. YEAH, IT GETS ONSHORE AND SMALL BUT THIS IS THE CLOSEST YOU'LL EVER GET TO RIDING THE SAME WAVE TWICE. IF YOU EVER HAVE A CHANCE TO GO THERE, DO IT BECAUSE IT'S THE MOST AMAZING PLACE TO FINE TUNE YOUR SURFING. HERE I RACED PAST A REO SECTION AND OPENED UP OFF THE WASH. WHAT A FEELING! WHAT A MANEUVER!

What's nice about backside roundhouse cutties is you don't need to twist your head to see where you're going. It's all there, right in front of you. Compared to a frontside cutback, you won't believe how easy these are to nail.

TO CUT IT OR CRACK IT?

▶ More often than not, doing a backside cutback means forfeiting a reo section in the process. You need to read what the section's about to do up ahead. Is it going to wall up quickly? Or is there enough time to race across it, double back, rebound off the foam, and still have enough speed to keep going? Usually the answer is obvious, as in this sequence. What else was I gonna do with that section? But there are times, you can't cutback without being left behind. Experience is the key to making the right decision. The more you practice, the sooner you'll get it.

Your first roundhouse cutback...

▶ First up: Forget a big bottom turn when entering the cutback. It's virtually impossible to come hard off the bottom, lay down a big powerful gouge, and still have enough speed to smash into the lip.

▶ To do a proper roundhouse, you need to move out on the face to get a full 180 in. Pump high to get wide, then start the turn like you're crouching into a frontside bottom turn. This starts to bring your board back around. Remember, keep the turn mellow at the start. This move is a bit of a two-step so you don't want to use up all your speed. Keep your weight even and start to look

up at that wall of foam. Wanna smack that thing, punk?

▶ When you see the foam, center yourself and aim for the spot you want to hit. Use all the speed you have left to hit it as high as you can. Tweak your ankles, give the back foot a little shove and your board will come up under you.

▶ Bouncing off the foam backside is so much easier than on a frontside cutback. You can get your weight on your heels and steer your board through the rebound. At first you'll bounce off the foam, and be stoked simply to have made the turn. But as you get better, you'll land in the pocket, ready to attack the next section. This rebound I'm doing here is fairly high. If you're only reaching the bottom of the wash, you're styling.

▶ As you improve, you can stand tall as you approach the foam and whack it high, turning it into a frontside reo. Eventually you'll be able to do the whole thing without losing any speed at all.

▶ Be careful about throwing a big roundhouse cutback on a barreling section. You can't bring it all the way around on a steep wave face and you'll end up taking on a pitching lip with everything going wrong. But that's cool. If it's steep, chuck a backside reo instead (see page 74).

▶ As you get better, you can start turning simple moves like this into something special. A case in point? The roundhouse cutback to reverse off the

foam. It sounds a mouthful but it's just an extension of a standoid b/s cutback. One of my local reef breaks, Bears, gets these really predictable lefts. I love easing out onto the face, aiming at the wash and coming off it with a frontside reverse (even though you're on a left!). Just adopt the same principles of a normal b/s cutback then hit the wash really low to help it spin. Do it quickly to get your board 'round backwards.

I love combining stuff. And so too will you.

TB TIP

TRAVEL DRUGS. I never use 'em but I want to because there's nothing worse than arriving somewhere out of your mind with fatigue. Flights over 12 hours really are torturous. If you can't sleep on planes, do yourself a favor and get some sleeping pills. Steer clear of over-the-counter pills, they don't always work and leave you groggy at the other end. Do it right, see a doctor. Get the goods and land fresh.

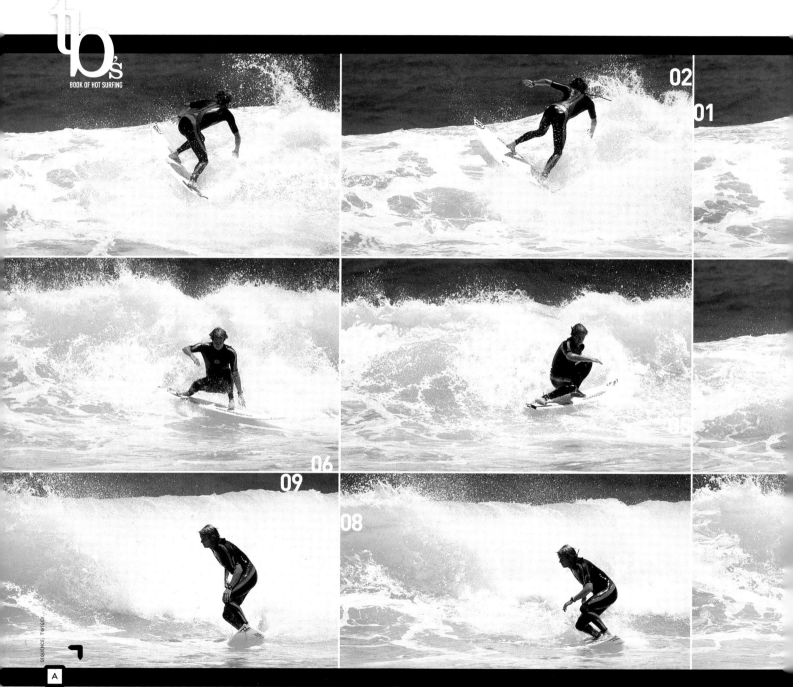

01

02

06

09

08

SEQUENCE: TWIGGY

A

A. TAKE IT NICE AND EASY. FOLLOW THE STEPS AND WATCH THE WORLD OF REVERSES AND AIR REVERSES TAKE HOLD. B. LOOK AFTER YOUR BOARDS AND CAR(S). NEGLECT 'EM AND CHANCES ARE THEY'LL LET YOU DOWN WHEN YOU REALLY NEED THEM.

BASIC 360

OKAY, YOU'RE NOT GONNA BELIEVE THIS BUT AFTER YOU LEARN AND CONQUER THE THREE-OH, YOU'LL LEAVE THAT TRICKY THING BEHIND. I SAY CONQUER, BECAUSE IF YOU'RE DEDICATED YOU WILL MAKE 360S. YOU'LL PUT YOURSELF INTO AN INITIAL FRENZY BUT THEN YOU'LL FORGET ABOUT IT.

See, the 360 opens a whole new world of maneuvers and once you get it, you move on. Think about it! The backside reverse is basically a frontside three-oh on your backhand! And the backside air-reverse! And the frontside floater three-oh!

ROUND WE GO...

▶ Wanna know the biggest mistake when you're learning to spin for the very first time? Most kids try to drive ridiculously off the bottom and attack the lip in some furious spinning motion. Most of the time they end up over the back of the wave.

▶ Your first 360 is a tough little thing to get your head around. You're not trying to spin all the way round, you're actually trying to do a 180. If you do this right, the wave's power will do the rest to spin you back around.

▶ Initially, the easiest way to spin is to use the whitewater. You need a moderately sloped face. If it's too steep, you'll end up going down the face backwards and smash into the trough. When it's fat, you'll be able to free up your fins and get halfway around.

▶ Getting the fins free is the key. I guess the best size wave to try is around two-to-three feet with a gentle sloping face. You need to cruise off the bottom and up the face. Don't try any crazy big bottom turn, alright?

▶ So, you're moving up the face, eyes on the little wash you've lined up. As you move up the face, your aim is to get on the wash. Just stay relaxed over the top of your board and then place some weight on your front foot.

▶ At the same time you need to put weight on your toeside rail to get a sliding motion going. Look down toward the wash where you've just come from and put pressure through your back foot and tail. Your board should free up.

▶ If you keep looking at the wash, you will most probably fall flat on your face as the board shoots from under your body.

▶ You need to keep your legs bent slightly, and keep your weight over your board. To spin to 360, you need to look toward the beach on your toeside rail. If you look over your shoulder to your heelside rail, there's a good chance you'll spin back the way you came.

▶ Also, you've gotta be careful how much weight you place on your back foot. Too much will sink your tail into the water and you'll get rolled. Too little and you'll drift over the back of the wave.

▶ The next part you won't be able to control in your early days. You're not used to your board spinning and almost kicking back. Whether you like it or not, it'll happen. Experience will teach your legs and body to get ready for the spin. It happens when your fins re-enter the water and grab. And there's nothing else to do but spin.

▶ Once you get the feel, you'll be able to try them straight on the face and you'll find they're not too tough.

▶ And just a hint, don't go trying them at the start of waves. You don't want to take off and fall off (you will) straight away and waste waves. You can try them on weaker closeouts. But more importantly, keep trying. You'll get em. They're the keys to most of the rest of this book.

TB TIP

WETTIE BUCKET. I always leave a block of wax in the car and get back there and it's melted into the carpet. It doesn't matter if your car isn't a Rolls Royce or Merc, wetsuit buckets are the go. You can pick them up from hardware stores or supermarkets for around 10 bucks. Salt water eats into your vehicle. Rust is cancer. They're also a good central storage place for wax, sunscreen and leggies.

B

B/S 360S, LIKE THE CHOP-HOP, ARE WHAT YOU KEEP IN YOUR BAG FOR THOSE MOMENTS WHEN A STANDARD REO OR CUTTY JUST ISN'T GOING TO CUT IT IN THE FUN STAKES. LIKE, THE WAVE'S DYING, YOU'RE STANDING THERE CRUISING ALONG, SCRATCHING YOUR HEAD... WHAT NOW? THROW THE TAIL OUT, TWIST THE SHOULDERS, TURN THE REVERSE LIGHTS ON, AND SPIN. B. TIE IT RIGHT AND IT WILL NEVER COME OFF.

BACKSIDE 360

THE BACKSIDE 360 IS, AT LEAST WHILE YOU'RE LEARNING, AN UNCONVENTIONAL MOVE. WHY DO 'EM WHEN YOU COULD THROW DOWN A REO OR LAUNCH YOURSELF INTO A CUTTY?

As you progress and get the feel of them though, you'll realize backside 360s are the keys to the city! They're actually the stepping stone to reverses, building blocks for even bigger and more beautiful moves. But for now, chill, learn the basics and move forward...

SPIN CITY...

▶ There's a few types of b'side three-o's but I'm gonna teach you the most basic and give you a few tips about the trickier spins downstairs.

▶ This is good move because it doesn't require much speed, the wind isn't a factor, and we've all got access to fat waves.

▶ Start your turn at the top of the wave. Ease yourself gently up the face. Do a serious bottom turn and it's all over.

▶ The key is lifting your fins out of the water to allow you to spin. By doing it at the top of a wave you'll have more chance of getting 'em free and then you'll have time to enjoy the ride and negotiate the spin back.

▶ Initially, you're going have to do something pretty dramatic so that your tail's facing the beach rather than your nose. How? Let's roll...

▶ You're at the top of the face. Providing there's no one in the way, look back over your shoulder toward the line-up. Here's where it gets heavy, but it reads tougher than it is. You've looked over, now at the same time lift your leading arm over your shoulder and move your back arm in the direction of the nose (like a cess slide on a skateboard) and push equal weight through your feet (heels, that is).

▶ Okay, you're sliding. You don't want to do a 180 and slide back the same way you came, so you need to look back over your shoulder toward the beach. It's a tired line but oh so true: where you look is where you go. During the backward stage keep all the weight on your front foot. If you add any weight on your back foot your fins will grab and you'll get rolled. It's a tough art but be sure to keep crouched and well balanced and use your back foot only as a rudder.

▶ This is the cool bit. Your board will spin automatically. Your momentum makes it happen. When you're learning you probably won't be able to control it and it'll spin and you'll fall. After you get the feel of the move pretty soon you'll learn the subtle weight transition of easing the weight back on your front foot as you spin around.

▶ Backside 360s get functional and more tech when you do them off the lip. That's when you can do a bottom turn and do it as a hitting-the-lip deal, even letting the fins flare out the back. Just remember at some point you have to slide. If you try to do a carving backside 360 then you're off track.

▶ The other three-o is when a wave closes out. If you've still got speed, you can bottom turn up over the wash and do the same things as listed above. First try doing it off little washes on the face. Sweaty!

TB TIP

TYING A LEASH STRING. Leash strings, the item that attaches your board to your leash are one of surfing's great wonders. Like wax, wax combs and sunscreen, they vanish without trace (though, there are some leash that have built in now)

So a few string rules... never use shoelaces as a long-term option – they will snap; never attach a string so long that it hangs off the rail. The rail saver (that piece with the velcro you wrap around the string) actually hangs over the rail, protecting it from nasty rope bites. If you don't want to buy a new leash just for the string (and what mad fool would), your local hardware store will be able to sort you out. Just buy a length of fine marine cord or similar, cut it to length and store the rest of the gear away in case of emergency.

B

A. BACKSIDE GRAB OVER THE POLE PRONG OF JOHN RESPONDEK. B. PICKING OVER THE BONES OF AN OLD FIRE. C. WITH STAMOS AND FELLOW WESTERN AUSTRALIAN KERBY BROWN. D. THE GENTLE GAME OF CRICKET WHEN THE AFTERNOON SOUTH-WESTER COMES UP. E. TIME AND CONVENTION MEAN LITTLE WHEN YOU'RE CAMPING IN AUSTRALIA'S NORTH-WEST. SAUSAGES FOR BREAKFAST, CEREAL BEFORE BED, WHATEVER WORKS. IT'S A FOCUSING EXPERIENCE LIVING AT A WORLD-CLASS WAVE – A TIME WHEN ALL THAT MATTERS IS YOUR SURFING , WHEN YOU LEARN TECHNIQUES AND SHARPEN MOVES THAT WILL SET YOUR STYLE UP FOR YEARS. F. RIDING IN THE 'CRUISER. BEATS PUMPING.

COOL STORY

TAJ RECALLS HIS FIRST MISSIONS TO WESTERN AUSTRALIA'S GREAT NORTH-WEST...

School vacations in winter are great if the oldies are switched on. Like, where do you want to go – the zoo or a trip up north where the waves break long and hard in warm water so clear you can watch turtles swim by?

Taj, whose parents are both keen surfers, wound up in the north-west each winter and can vividly recall his fourth birthday at The Bluff, near Carnarvon.

"We went to hang out at the Bluff before there was anyone there really. My tent was one of those little foldout tables with a little tarp hanging over it! That was my little tent! So crook!" says Taj. "They just had their tent and we were just groveling. I didn't even surf, I just used to play on the beach with my little toy cars and stuff and they used to argue over who had to look after me while they surfed. I was just kicking at a campfire, my dad playing guitar and my mom used to bring a little set of fricken congos and start jamming out. Biggest hippies. They still do the same thing now."

His standout sesh from the early days? "I remember one session I was about 11 surfing this left called Birdy Creek and it was, like, four foot and I remember I had a 5'8" gun and it had this red rail spray on it. I kept thinking 5'8" was way too big a board to turn and I just ended up really liking it. I remember doing these two backhand floaters in a row and right when *Kelly Slater in Black and White* had come out and I was just thinking I was Kelly at Restaurants. It felt like I'd done the exact same thing like he did and my dad was loving it going, 'They were the best two floaters I've ever seen' and I was just going, 'YEAH!!!' I was so psyched and it was the best little trip and he was just raving to all his mates how good I was surfing and I was just so stoked. I felt like the sickest little dude ever. It was bullsh**t."

You're wondering how the kid got so good in lefts? Thank his parents.

TB TIP

GOOD TUNES. Make sure you've always got good music on road trips. Mix tapes or burnt discs are the go. I'm freaking on Ipods right now. I love the technology wizardry. My Ipod can hold 5000 songs and it's the same size as a mini disc. I love all music and it changes so much. Today, right now, November 25 2002 at Off the Wall in Hawaii, this is my list... The Vines, Iggy pop, Chili Peppers and Outkast.

A. WANT TO SHOW THE LINE-UP WHAT YOUR FINS LOOK LIKE? GET A FRONTSIDE WAFT INTO YOUR REPERTOIRE. B. WHEN YOU FEEL THE BLUR, NECK SOME GRITS AND POUR DOWN THE WATER.

FRONTSIDE WAFT

[OR FRONTSIDE FINS-OUT REO] PG // 105

YOU'LL EXPERIENCE DIFFERENT KINDS OF MATES BUT THE ONES WHO COMPLIMENT YOUR TURNS WILL ALWAYS BE ONES YOU'LL TRY TO SURF WITH. IT'S NOT AN EGO THING, IT'S JUST NICE TO RECIPROCATE COMPLIMENTS AND APPRECIATE PEOPLE'S SURFING.

Mates who pretend they didn't see a turn suck. If I'm in the water and someone does a psycho turn, I'll hoot or tell 'em it looked pretty sweaty. If a mate is paddling over the wave and you're about to smack the lip, it's so inviting to throw your tail as high as you can so the person can see all three fins. I love that feeling. I just want to get the whole fricken tail out with a big blast. Wanna do one? Come with me...

THREE ON THE TREE...

▶ If you're on this page then you probably know how to do a standard frontside reo. The standoid reo usually means you point the nose of the board toward the lip, move up the face and when your board is hit by the lip it changes your direction and you're sent back down the face.

▶ The weird thing about wafts is that you may have already done them and not realized. I've often done frontside reos, gone home and seen the turns on video and they've been wafts and some even looked like airs! Thing is, your mates might have seen your fins from behind but be too rattled to tell you. Anyway, right now let's pretend you've never done one.

▶ Wafting is a reo where you do a kind of rail-slide on the lip when your fins hang out the back of the wave.

▶ Okay, what you're looking for is a lip just about to break, a crumbly section for you to climb up and follow through with your tail. The good thing about these is that you can waft almost regardless of the wind so you can get real tricky in the onshore slop.

▶ You can practice on closeouts and this will ensure you've always got a section. But they look best when you do them on the face and ride into the next turn. So, looking for the right closeout is the key: not too sucky otherwise you'll find yourself getting stuck in the trough.

▶ For a good waft, you need a decent amount of speed. Not as much speed as an air but enough to get your board and body above the lip, so you get over it and can make it. Initially try it on waves that aren't too steep. If there's a section where you could get barreled and you try a massive waft, you'll probably get smoked.

▶ As you bottom turn, look at the crumbly lip you want to hit. It's an oldie but true: where you look is where you go. You can adopt a little wider stance than normal, one foot right back on your tail and the other in the middle of the board is cool for me. You need to be fairly compressed during the bottom turn as you want to extend up the face to hit the lip. As you move up the face pull your board under your feet and extend toward the lip. At the start, you'll probably come up too late or too early but if you do, you can still do a good turn without wafting, so it's a nice reliable turn.

▶ As you hit the lip, you need to become weightless and pivot on the lip. When you feel the lip connect with your board, you need to twist your body and push your tail. If you push too hard you'll flick out and fall backwards, and if you don't push enough, you'll probably do some gammy jive on the lip. Once you get the feeling up there, you'll know what feels good.

▶ If you've made reverses before, the weightless feeling will be similar. The key is to get a little sideways but now it gets tricky. You're at the wave's mercy. Your fins are free of water and when your fins grab it's the wave's say. You have to be prepared for the board to grab at any time, so you need to have weight on your back foot.

▶ Just to mix up your vernacular, pronounce waft as it's spelt. Rather than "woft" accentuate the "a" to "waff-t".

TB TIP

NECKED? Before you go to bed after a night on the juice, force yourself to eat and drink. I rarely think clearly in the necked state, and at the time there's nothing worse, but get some grits and plenty of water down your gills. Next day you'll feel craploads better. And if you don't? Fight it. Surf, swim, just get out of bed and the house.

B

STEVE SHERMAN

WILD BACKSIDE WAFT

[AND SOME GEAR ON HAWAII]

WILD BACKSIDE WAFTS LIKE THIS ONE ARE KINDA DIFFICULT TO EXPLAIN. SEEING THIS ONE WENT DOWN IN HAWAII, I'M GOING TO TELL YOU A LITTLE ABOUT HAWAII, A LITTLE BIT ABOUT THE BACKSIDE FIN THROW. COOL? GOOD...

HAWAII'S CROWDED...

For more than six months of the year, the North Shore doesn't break. And when those rare swells squeak through in the downtimes, the reefs are filled with sand and the waves are generally crook. Come October, when the waves start to turn on, almost every pro surfer in the world rocks up to this tiny stretch of coast. Locals are keen, and they charge, so lineups are quickly filled. Couple this with your own fear of the ocean's might and you're not getting too many waves. Tips? Surf early. Most tend to lag and the photo sluts can't shoot without sunlight.

The wave's pump

But do you need to attack this stretch of coast? Well, as a surfer, at some point, you should. The waves pack way more punch and power and intensity than anywhere in the world, but it seems kinda silly to me – you could get way more barrels somewhere else with less people. Ride a normal short board on the North Shore and you'll feel the power. I've surfed five or six feet Off the Wall and if I was surfing the same size waves back at home, I'd be riding a 5'11" – 6'1" max – and be dropping in no worries. Over there, it's strictly the 7'0" barge club!

And the reef is evil

And there are caves. The best thing about this waft is that it was at Log Cabins. After all the reef warrior work you do in Hawaii this is the North Shore's beachie. You can be less cautious out there and throw some bigger turns.

So waft over it

▶ The best lips are nice and crumbly. The backside waft, more than any other turn, is about timing. Go up too early and you'll get hung up and have nothing to grind across. Too dumpy and you're toast. Too fat and the wave won't let you have a coping to grind across.

▶ Most of the time I can do a reo and know why I'm doing it, what variations leave different outcomes. Here, well, I just stuff my head toward my legs and kick my tail out. The weight on your back foot shouldn't be too heavy, more on your front so you can pivot the tail. The more you push the more you'll slide.

▶ I rarely use it but I see guys like Stamos grab their inside rail when they do a backside waft. It's a good because this chills out the sliding and stabilizes you for exit out of the turn.

▶ The backside fin throw is where you get hung up in the lip most. You do your snap, have too much weight on your back foot, and get stuck in the lip. Getting hung up shits me more than anything. I just bail out. It's not even worth making it. You never get around the section and are lured.

▶ Backside wafts look so sick from the water. I see some sometimes, then check the footage and they're just rude. I like Andy's the best. He does them most accurately. You know he's gonna make it. Real life or video, his are sweet.

Hawaiian vibes

It's heavy. When I was about 17, I was sent in at Velzyland. This huge guy paddled right up to me and I thought he was gonna smack me in the head but he just smashed the water right in front of my face. Last season, a guy got annihilated for an accidental drop-in. You learn the lessons hard in Hawaii. The East and West sides are heavy too. You just gotta be careful or surf small ordinary days like this one at Log Cabins. Even those days pack plenty of power to get loose.

Girls

There never used to be any at all, just a couple of real lucky ones, ha ha, some popular ones. But the past few years there've been lots of girls, some really cute girls. And, uh, that's a lot of fun.

The verdict

If you're on the gravy train like I am it's good to stay on the beach at Pipe and wake up and see it all take place in front but if I didn't have to surf over there I wouldn't. Some people love it but the moment the comps are over, I'm out.

TB TIP

THE GREAT INK DEBATE. Just recently, I've felt pretty close to getting a tatt. I'm inkless and after talking to a few people I just feel like getting one. They were like, "If I was you and I never had to work a normal job I'd be getting the sickest ink. I can't go and do it and go and try and get a job." It's such a gnarly thing to do and it'd need to be something pretty special. I just can't imagine getting something and two weeks later going, "Oh no, what is this rank bit of art on me?"

A

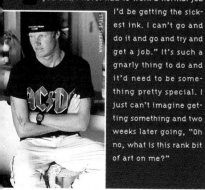

A. PURE MUSCLE, PEN TATTS AND ACCA DACCA ATTITUDE. OH, AND DON'T FORGET THE TRANSWORLD HAT B. YOU GET TO THE LIP, YOU'RE STILL IN CONTROL AND YOU CAN JUST KICK THAT TAIL. TB THROWS A WILD SNAP AT LOG CABINS IN HAWAII, DECEMBER 2002.

01

03

05

07

SEQUENCE: BOSKO.

A

A. THE IN-THE-POCKET FRONTSIDE HACK. PERFECT FOR SHOWERING ANY SHOULDER HOPPERS WITH YOUR FILTHY, FOAMY SCUM. B. STAMOS SUBMITS TO TAJ'S HAIR-CUTTING INEXPERTISE.

FRONTSIDE HACK

OKAY, SO YOUR CALF MUSCLES ARE NO THICKER THAN YOUR ANKLES. DON'T SWEAT IT, YOU CAN STILL SURF WITH POWER. HERE'S A BIG STATEMENT: SKINNY PEOPLE ARE BETTER POWER SURFERS.

Think about it. If you've got a small build, you need a better technique to move the same amount of water. Big guys don't need to put as much into it as you to get big results. Watch them surf and you'll see how easily they move water. Far better, though, to do it with finesse.

ANYWAY, LET'S WET THOSE RAILS...

▶ Sick of my saying this? Yep, you need speed. You can be going fairly slow and still do a frontside hack but, to really impress, to get those "whooaaarrs!" from the beach, you need speed.

▶ A hack is basically a cutback without the rebound. You know, the figure-eight motion.

▶ So, wetting the rails and making it rain on the guys out the back goes a little something like this. Check out the first frame, my front foot is in the centre of my board, my back foot is right back on the tail and my front arm is telling me where I want to go. Here we go again: where you look, and where your arms point, is where you go. You're learning, aren't you?

▶ As you bottom turn, most of your weight should be on your back foot and the pressure should be placed on your toes on your front. This will bring you up the face.

▶ You can hack anywhere on a wave but the most explosive and most satisfying is high up the face. It's where the wave is steeper, so it's not as easy, but boy oh boy does it look the goods. If you do it right, you'll even flash a little fin to the kids out the back.

▶ Look closely at when I get to the top of the wave. This is where you should change everything. Pull your arms back under your body really quickly, and look down to where you want to go. The quicker you do this change, the more intense the turn. The actual turning motion sometimes involves a little head flick, which feels really good. You've changed direction, you've got foam all around and you're throwing buckets. A dynamic little head twist adds to the sensation.

▶ Anyway, you've got body torque sorted. See what your feet are doing. When you've done the hack, all your weight will wind up on the heel of your front foot. This transfer of weight pushes your board the way your body is twisted. Remember the old Billabong video with Occy doing the frontside hack and his toes aren't even on his board? Well, that's what I'm talking about. Heel, brudda, plenty of heel.

▶ You've done the turn, now you gotta get out of there. This is where your arms come into play, again. You've gotta use the wash to get you out of there. Use them to support you.

▶ The key is to stay over your board. When you lay back, you need to let the wash pick you up. Lean back over your tail, not the inside rail. You'll find it easier to get back up. You can avoid the layback if you don't drive all the way to the bottom of the wave, but the harder you push it, the better it looks.

▶ I guess it's better to do the full-blown hack at the end of a wave. If you do it on a really good wave that keeps

walling up, there's a good chance you won't get back around the wash. A good hack is impressive with crowds and all, but not if it means the rest of the wave peels off unridden.

TB TIP

CUTTING HAIR. An old saying, there's only two weeks between a good haircut and a bad haircut. Messy hair's in right now and that's our saving grace.

So, straight hair, you're in trouble. Twist the hair in your fingers and cut at a 45 degree angle. Apply technique all the way round until it's fairly even.

Curly hair. Mow that crap. It hides chunks especially when you're using the angled cutting explained above.

Every other hair. Ah, who cares, let two weeks deal with it! Shave it if it's too bad and ride the kudos train as a cat who isn't vain and doesn't care about his hair (for two weeks anyway.)

04

B

globe

A TAJ LETS HIS WINGS OUT AT A BEACHBREAK A LONG WAY FROM HIS HOMETOWN, YALLINGUP, WESTERN AUSTRALIA

HOW TO

AVOID BEING A FILTHY RACIST [BY DEREK RIELLY] PG // 111

THERE'S A LOT OF DIFFERENT PEOPLE IN THIS WIDE WORLD, ARE YOU COOL ENOUGH TO ACCEPT 'EM ALL?

Holy crap, what's gone wrong with the western democracies? One minute we're the coolest countries on earth, places that welcome the tortured masses from all those countries with rank dictators, next we're sticking 'em in jail as illegal immigrants.

Eighty-eight Australians were murdered in Bali and the papers ran tributes, we talked of 'em as heroes, yet when nearly 400 refugees, including children, drowned off our northern coast en route to better lives in Australia all we did was breathe a collective sigh that we didn't have to take any more.

It's hard to accept difference. Most wars are fought because two sides didn't like the others' religion or the way they comb the hair or something ridiculous. As a surfer, the world is yours and every person a potential friend. Here's some tips to avoid awakening the racist inside us all.

1. Travel. The more you get outside your suburb, the more you'll realize how alike we all are. You might even discover that Americans or Australians aren't the coolest people in the world afterall and that there are some countries you'd dig living in.

2. Read about different cultures. White American and Australian histories are short, there's people out there who are the product of thousands of years of wars and revolutions.

3. Learn a language or two. It isn't as hard as you might think, although it does take time and patience, and, suddenly, you won't be describing foreign language as gibberish any more.

4. Every man needs to make love to all the colors of the rainbow. Can't do that if you're racist, can you?

5. Avoid getting your opinions from tabloid newspapers (the smaller ones). They're festering pits of reactionary politics and only feed a society's prejudice and fear.

6. Got a problem with refugees? Visit a detention center, talk to a kid your own age and find out all the s**t he had to get through just so he could land himself, innocent and uncharged, in a western jail.

7. Don't judge people as groups or stereotypes. Go to Lebanon or Cairo, for instance, and you'll be surprised how cool and warm and amazing they and their country is.

8. Describing someone as black or Asian doesn't make you a racist. Dropping N-Bombs outside of a hip-hop track does.

TB TIP

SCRAP MERCHANT. It's so easy, when you're sitting in a pack, to paddle with the crowd when a set comes, hoping you'll be the one to get a piece of the bigger action. But look around you first. While everyone's eyes are fixed on the waves behind, what's going on in the foreground? Is there a little one that everyone has overlooked? If so, snap it up. A guaranteed smaller wave is often better than gambling on taking a set wave from the crowd. This is just one advantage of not going with the flock. Paddle in the opposite direction from everyone else and you will pick up the juicy scraps the others can't even see — crazy little double-ups that the guys out the back can't get on to, little walls that don't closeout, reforms and wedges. Don't just sit around waiting with everyone else, keep sniffing.

02

03

05

04

08

07

SEQUENCE: TWIGGY.

A

A. WHAT A JOY TO HIT THAT WASH, KICK OUT THE TAIL AND LET THE FOAM DO ALL THE WORK. CHECK HOW TAJ'S WEIGHT IS CENTRED OVER THE FRONT FOOT KEEPING THE FINS FROM DIVING INTO THE WASH. B. LOW-LEVEL CRIMINAL ACTIVITIES AT THEIR BEST: TB AND RADAR DETECTOR.

FRONTSIDE REVERSE

WHEN I STARTED DOING REVERSES, I'D DO WHAT I'M DOING IN THIS SEQUENCE: GRAB MY RAIL, TURN OFF THE FOAM. THING WAS, THEY WERE SUCH SMALL WAVES THAT I'D BE GOING BACKWARDS FOR AGES IN THE WASH, PADDLING WITH MY ARMS TRYING TO STAY WITH THE WAVE AND SPIN.

Now I do them easier and a bit faster on more critical sections. But I still grab my rail, Andy Irons-style. People ask me who did the grab-rail reverses first, me or Andy? I've got no idea but all I know is they look sick and they feel even better.

FINS OUT, JOIN THE MERRY GO ROUND...

▶ A reverse is not a 360. A 360 you turn off your inside or toeside rail. A reverse you turn off you heelside rail, even though you spin like a 360.

▶ What's cool about reverses is you don't need a whole heap of speed. So don't do a strong bottom turn, just ease up the face because you need to get your entire board and body around. And don't go all vertical on me either. As any snowboarders reading this'll know, the key to spins off the lip (in their case, jumps) is to begin your turn early. See in the sequence how I hit the lip with my board almost horizontal to the lip.

▶ As you approach a soft, foamy section start your turn at the top of the wave. When your board hits the wash, the foam should loosen up the fins and you'll start to slide. Also, if you're already turning you've already started the motion of getting around before you hit the wash. Basically, a frontside reverse is backside 360 on your forehand. Have a think about that

▶ At this stage, or until you start moving down the face, you need to keep the weight on your back foot. With weight on the front foot, you'll head down the wave too quickly and probably fall off. With plenty of prac-

tice you'll soon realise that by the bottom of the wave you'll need to adjust your weight to your front foot so your fins don't dig in.

▶ As soon as you hit the bottom of the wave your board will spin. This is because your fins have essentially been out of the water (well, in the wash. No traction) and as soon as they grab their tendency is to spin you around.

▶ Whichever shoulder you look over is the way you'll turn. Sometimes I'll be going backwards and I'll be around straight really quickly and people think I did a reverse when it was a standard backward reo.

▶ Also, when you get better and know how to move your weight you'll be able to do reverses off the bottom of the wash. These happen quickly and take a good deal of skill but the theory's the same.

▶ As you get better and hit the lip vertically, you'll notice the subtleties with weight. You'll hit the lip, push with your back foot then immediately have weight on your front foot. It's a fun park out there, readers.

TB TIP

I'M GOING TO SOUND LIKE THE FULL SPEED NUT HERE. MAYBE I AM. LIKE, I SURE DIG MY 700-BUCK RADAR DETECTOR.

I lost my license a few years ago and it was heavy. It was the same time I had a bung ankle and I honestly had nothing to do. Drive and surf, that's all I pretty much do. Not only was I on the grief train I was driver and conductor. So, after that I picked up this radar detector. It's saved me so many times. I'm not a crazy speed fiend or anything but this thing is gold when I'm going like 20 clicks over the speed limit. And, best of all, I've still got a license.

B

SURFING BIG WAVES

I'M NOT TRYING TO FREAK YOU OUT OR ANYTHING BUT SURFING BIG WAVES IS SERIOUS. YOU PADDLE INTO A WAVE AND IF YOU MAKE ANY MISTAKE, IT FEELS AS IF THE ENTIRE OCEAN IS GONNA STOMP YOU INTO A PREMATURE GRAVE.

You need total faith in your equipment. Think you can take your trusty 6'2" out in any size surf and still rule? Listen to this.

In the 1999 Pipe Masters, I was so psyched. I was up against Kalani Robb and Tamayo Perry and knew it'd be a tough one to take out. So, I'm out there and I'd had a good wave over at Pipe and was paddling into a bomb at Backdoor. It was a real late drop but I got into the wave okay because I paddled really hard. I was getting excited and thought, "Here we go, this thing's 10 points for sure." I held my line but my board had different ideas and started tracking! It couldn't hold its line in the tube and I was in a massive cave at Backdoor Pipe. The board was pulled from under my feet and I couldn't pen-

etrate the water, then... fump! The next thing I know my ass was slammed against the reef and my back was laid out. My mind raced... was I paralysed? Was this it? I came up and the sets keep bombing my head. Usually I would've been freaked, but in this spaced-out state, I was cool. I wasn't worried and was dealing with wearing these things on the head. I got washed in, walked a few paces up the beach and just... collapsed. I couldn't walk and I felt weird and just had to lie there. Everyone surrounded me and I was just spinning out! The next thing I knew I was being stretchered into the back of an ambulance. I was being offered morphine and I was totally strapped in. I had straps around my head, my legs, my arms, my hips, I couldn't move and I was desperately trying to test my limbs to see if I was paralysed. Then I get to Wahiawa hospital and the pain was like nothing I've ever felt and I was wishing I had stepped up to the morphine. I was so freaked but I got the x-rays and everything was cool. They gave me a heap of anti-inflammatories and a pillow to sit on and I got outta there in Kalani's clothes (turned out he gave me his when I got in the ambo). Then on the way back to my crib I found out I won the heat.

The comp was on hold for the next week and a week later I was back out Pipe in a man-on-man heat with Tamayo. I was just too rattled to go right. The memory of the pain and the fear was still with me. And trying to beat Tamayo at Pipe is just impossible.

Tamayo smoked me.

BELIEVE IN YOUR ABILITY...

Surfing big waves is something you have to do if you want to be a complete surfer. The best thing about big waves is that there's guys out there who may not surf amazing but come into this superleague of their own when the waves get up. Their awkward styles suddenly evaporate and they look more like surfers than any kid throwing 360s in the shorebreak.

▶ Many believe that even the most average surfer can tackle big waves. I disagree. It's easy to say all you have to do is paddle and stand up but when the horizon goes black and what looks like the the entire ocean stands up in front of you, it takes an above-average surfer to spin and have a shot at taking off.

▶ I don't think there's a person in the world that doesn't have the butterflies run into their stomach when they're surfing big waves. And that's not such a bad thing. Treat it in the right way and you'll convince yourself your body is tuning up, readying itself for the ride of a lifetime.

▶ Don't ever hesitate. Breathe heavily through your nose. Snarl and grunt if you have to but as soon as you paddle, know you're going to go. Paddle harder than you ever have before. There are two reasons for this. One, because speed equals stability and will make the drop easier and, two, is to let the other guys in the line-up know you're serious. If you pull back, it's likely you won't get another bite at a set.

▶ Use the hoots from other guys in

the line up to fire you up. All their focus is on you. You're on centre stage! It's your turn to get noticed! Imagine the hero you'll become if you make it. And want to know the quickest way to get respect in a crowded line-up? Charge.

▶ Don't be stupid. Don't paddle out and try to take off under the lip of an ugly wedge. Take what you know you're going to make.

▶ When you're paddling, put your mind through the motions of success. Think about riding the wave out. Negatives don't exist. The moment you think about getting licked, you'll eat it.

▶ If the waves are big at home or at a wave you feel comfortable with, it'll reflect in your confidence. If I know the waves are big at my home break I sprint to the beach so quick that I could easily go out with my leash on the wrong foot I'm so excited.

▶ Hawaii is a lot different. It wakes you up in the middle of the night. It's like the islands are shaking and you're laying in bed, trying to sleep and your brain's going, "Ohh s**t, here we go." When I wake I just cruise down to the beach and take it nice and easy. Breathe deeply. Watch the sets, where guys are paddling, clean-up sets, where I'd get in and what I'd do if I lost my board. I take my time. You are going to get worked, so you need to work out how to make sure it happens as little as possible.

▶ Ultimately, if you've been true to yourself and have not talked yourself out of taking off, you'll be so stoked. It's all about getting your head around it and once you've taken that first heavy drop, the cards will all fall into place.

TB TIP

SAVING COIN. Eat at home, not out. Do bakeries, not cafes. Burn CDs off your friends, don't lay down 20 skins. Don't let money-saving rule your life but go easy. Scrooges suck. Kids who take caution are cool.

A

DA PIPE.

riding a good reliable 7'6". pipe is no
place to test out some new dodgey craft.

25 ft.

i wish i could call this a 25 ft
wave, but actually only considered

12 ft. due to the 'macho' system,

Surfing man on man
heats @ pipe is pretty
special, any other day 50
guys would be hunting
this peak

Should hit it or
stall for the pit →
but i don't think
i did.

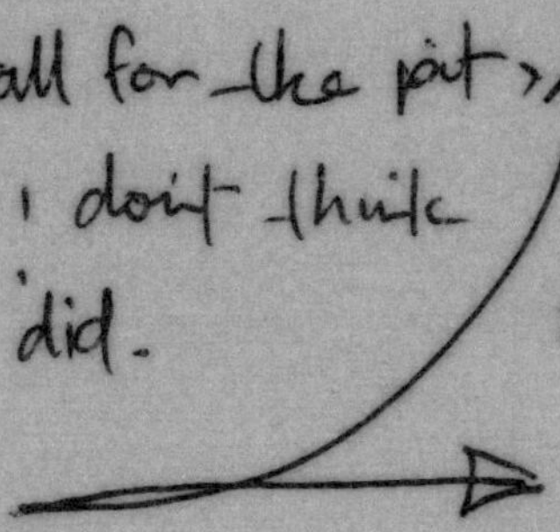

most likely
raced out onto the
shoulder for 2.0
points.

DA PIPE.

25 ft. ⌐

riding a good reliable 7.6'. pipe is no
place to test out some new dodgey craft.

I wish i could call this a 25ft
wave, but actually only considered

but i don't think
i did.

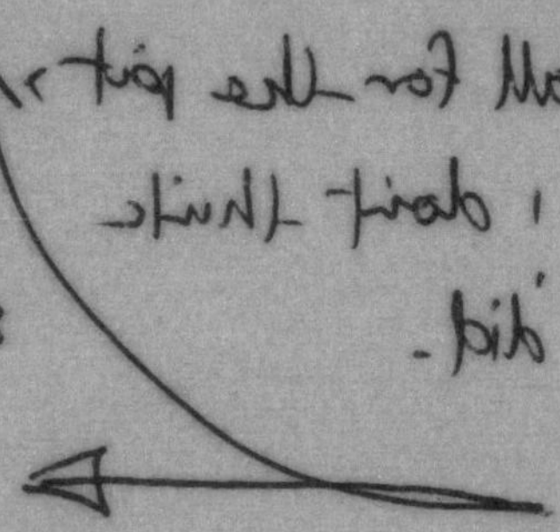

most likely
raced out onto the
shoulder for 20
this peak

A. EATING AT HOME — FASTER, CHEAPER AND HEALTHIER (USUALLY) THAN THE GEAR YOU'LL GET AT THE STORE. B. DRAWING A LONG BOTTOM TURN IN THE MAW OF A SET AT PIPELINE, ON OAHU'S NORTH SHORE. ONE OF SURFING'S GREAT THRILLS.

BACKSIDE REVERSE

KELLY DID THE FIRST DOCUMENTED REVERSE IN THE EARLY 1991 PROFILE MOVIE, *KELLY SLATER IN BLACK AND WHITE*. SOME SAY HE WAS THE FIRST, OTHERS ARGUE CHRISTIAN FLETCHER OR SOME OBSCURE LOCAL HERO.

Know what? I don't really care. All I know is Kelly's were intentional and they freaked out everyone. (And I mean everyone 'cause his vid was 10 bucks when the rest were 30, and everyone

02

03

TB TIP

PERSISTENCE CAN BE THE KEY. I'm in a different situation to you but if my shortboard's not going so well, I just get rid of it. I think I've gotten confident enough to make that decision early. Seeing you probably don't get as many boards as I do, you don't have that luxury. Boards can be an acquired taste. You just have to keep riding it to feel different things. The immediate reason you probably don't like a board is because it feels different to anything you've ever ridden. If you ride it enough, you'll feel the finer details, the way it moves in fat waves. And if you don't, then you might have to keep riding it because it's all you got.

A

RESPONDER

owned it.) Because of the spin, the section of the vid was called *Reverse*, and ever since then, the name has since stuck like glue.

Before we get started, there's a few things you should know about backside reverses. Throwing 'em on the face is really lame. It's easy to ride a tiny board and let the board spin under your feet. But a maneuver like that will probably only bring you ridicule. The key is to do them after a full-rail cutback, as a committed reo or as a way to deal with a chubby cutback. This one's at a little left near my house called Mamas.

POWER AND CONFIDENCE...

▶ For starters, you need to be more committed than usual. You need to do the turn and then some. You can do them after cutbacks, on whitewash or on a closeout. But my favorite is to do it as a reo.

▶ Okay, the bottom turn. Look up at the lip like you're doing a standard reo. Raise your back arm to the wave and your body will twist and send the nose of your board up the face.

▶ Here's where you have to start to think you're going to do a reverse. When you reach the top of the wave your weight should still be on the back foot. From here, you need to pivot and put the 360 part in.

▶ You need to crouch and put all of your power into the turn. You might see in this sequence that I've buried my head into the wash. What I've done here is put my weight onto my front foot so I can free up my fins and do the spin. If your fins are totally in the water

it'll be tough to spin.

▶ When you feel your fins come free, you should already be backwards, so you need to remain balanced. If you keep your face in the wash or toward your tail, you will seriously reduce your chance of making it. So pull your head out and look over your shoulder. Looking that way will also make sure you spin to reverse and back the normal way.

▶ As a rule, where you look is where you go. If you're looking down the wave, that's where you're gonna head. Unless everything happens too quickly for you, you'll probably make it.

▶ When you feel your board spin around, move your weight to the back foot again so you don't lose control and spin out.

▶ To get the real feel go for really committed backside reos. You'll spin but usually spin off the back. This is good and will get you used to the feeling of spinning and what you're doing wrong. Remember, *always remember*, where you look is where you go and you can't go wrong.

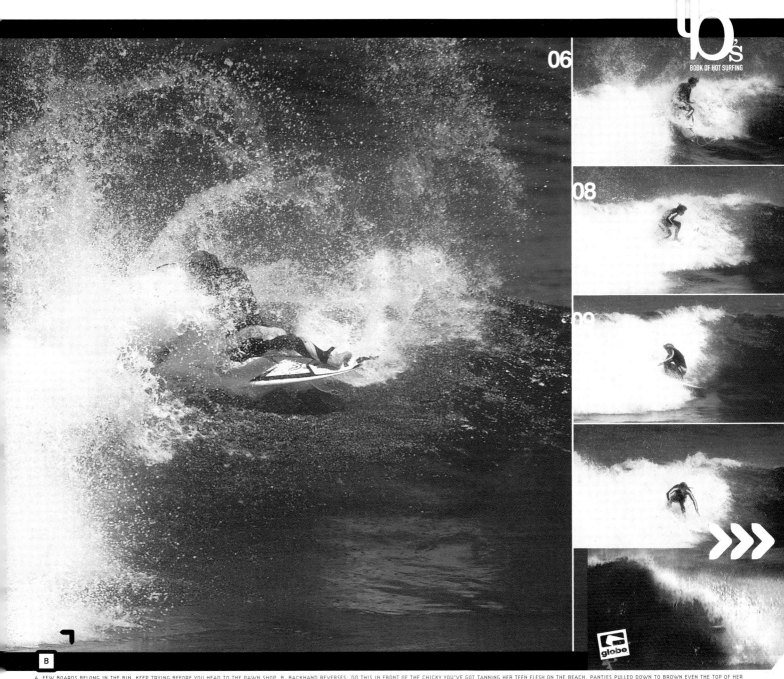

B

A. FEW BOARDS BELONG IN THE BIN. KEEP TRYING BEFORE YOU HEAD TO THE PAWN SHOP. B. BACKHAND REVERSES: DO THIS IN FRONT OF THE CHICKY YOU'VE GOT TANNING HER TEEN FLESH ON THE BEACH, PANTIES PULLED DOWN TO BROWN EVEN THE TOP OF HER HUMP, AND SHE'LL ADORE YOU FOR LIFE.

A

A. GIVEN ITS SIMPLICITY - WEIGHT ON FRONT FOOT, BACK FOOT STEERS, BODY SQUARED – IT'S ASTONISHING HOW FEW SURFERS CAN RIDE TUBES ON THEIR BACKHAND. BUT WHEN ALL THE ELEMENTS DO COME TOGETHER, USUALLY ON A HOLIDAY TO INDONESIA, AND YOU JAG A TUBE AND LET YOUR BODY CURVE TO THE WAVE, THERE'S NO SWEETER FEELING OF ACCOMPLISHMENT. B. WEST AUSTRALIA'S HEAVIEST WAVE AND SOME RELAXED THREADING CONSIDERING THE SIZE.

BACKSIDE TUBERIDING

BACKSIDE TUBERIDING IS ONE OF THE TOUGHEST THINGS TO MASTER IN THIS CRAZY LITTLE ART OF WAVE RIDING. I WASN'T SURE WHAT SECTION TO PUT THIS INTO BECAUSE I KNOW GUYS WHO DON'T SURF THAT GREAT WHO ARE AMAZING BACKSIDE TUBERIDERS.

01

04

05

SEQUENCE. TWIGGY.

B

Personally, I've still got a lot to learn. They're just so... fricken... awkward. I always struggled like most people do but in the past few years I've gotten more of a feel of it from surfing places like Macaronis in Indo.

TWIST THAT BODY...

▶ Your first tube will blow your mind. All those other times when you thought you were in the tube and you raced onto the shoulder and laid down a big roundhouse cutback in celebration will be remembered with quite a laugh.

▶ It's the whole unknown of having your back to the wave, twisting and the feeling that you're gonna fall forward when you get clipped. One of the hardest things to do is touch the wave's face as you lean against it with your hand in the wave. You've got to make your body so it fits the curve and keep yourself planted

There are a few different style of backside tuberiding...

▶ **Pigdog.** The pigdog is the most common style of backside tube riding. The name came about 'cause most guys get this rank dog face on 'em. What you do is ride with your back knee almost dropped to the board, your back arm on the rail and your front arm running along the face.

▶ **Pigdog with stall.** This is the perfect way to ride the tube for as long as possible. Lean into the face with your hip and front arm. Sometimes I find it hard to do this without spraying myself in the face.

▶ **Hands on deck.** This approach has you leaning forward with both hands on the deck of your board. It's good for really fast tubes but you're not as stable. You'll rock around and can get clipped easily.

▶ **Lay forward grabrail.** Lean forward, grab your outside rail with your back hand and look up at the lip. Luke Egan does this one really well.

▶ **No hands.** I reckon you need big open tubes to ride no hands but the Hobgoods master it in, like, three-foot tubes. The holy grail of b/s tuberiding, as far as I'm concerned. Amazing.

▶ **Layback.** The old-school Ross Clarke-Jones style. No rail grab, just your whole back fitting the curve of the wave. Your trailing arm and shoulder guides you in the tube.

▶ Pig dogging from the take-off is easier than surfing along the wave, lining up a section, grabbing the rail and setting up the tube.

▶ At the start, you'll pig dog and the lip will hit you in the side of the head. When this happens I can almost guarantee your front hand wasn't on the face.

▶ The way to succeed is to get in your stance as soon as you stand up. Eventually what you'll want to do is slide down the face. The challenge is to distribute the weight between your feet. Too much weight on your front foot, the foam will hit you, the fins will come free and you'll slide out in the tube. Too much weight on your back foot, you'll get hung up on the face, clipped in the head and launched over the falls.

▶ Like all tubes, one of the biggest problems is jumping off too early. You're in the tube, it's the safest part of the wave, why would you want to get outta that groovy town? Because it's scary in those early days. It's heavy, I know. It feels as though your head is gonna be driven into the surface below. And these wipeouts happen so easily. Go too high, you can't correct and you get tossed forward. Too low and you're gone under the lip.

▶ Whether you know it or not, your back foot sits real close to the outside rail, while your front foot sits close to the inside rail up front. They balance each other out.

▶ Practice in beachies where the consequences aren't too serious.

TB TIP

PARKING THE CAR OUT OF SIGHT... Will be common. When you're in the surf and you have no idea what could happen to your car, make sure there's nothing inside. If you've got an extra board, it's way safer speared into the sand on the beach.

globe

A. EYES ON THE LIP, ARMS POISED. SOMETIMES TUBERIDING CAN BE A SERIOUS BUSINESS. TAJ SURFS AT MUFFLERS, THE WAVE THAT BROKE A GOOD SURFER'S NECK. B. THE ACCEPTED WAY OF HOLDING YOUR CRAFT. RANK SQUAT OPTIONAL.

HEAVY STORY

TAJ'S FIRST-HAND EXPERIENCE OF A QUICK WIPEOUT THAT LEFT A GOOD SURFER UNABLE TO SURF AGAIN.

Surfing backside tubes is dodgy. Listen: I was surfing this ledging little right reef a few years ago not too far from my place. It was only about three feet, the water was blue, the sun was shining and this dude paddled out up the inside. He kept paddling deeper on the inside and a really nice one came through. He was too deep but took it anyway. It's a tough wave to surf backside and I knew he was going to be too deep and I was kinda angry because it was such a good little wave. I remember thinking, "I shoulda gone that thing". But he made the drop and I saw him try to pull up under the lip, get clipped and then get sucked over the falls headfirst right at the shallowest spot. Right then, my anger disappeared because I knew something gnarly had just gone down. Surfing injuries are rare but sometimes you just know. I was looking in to see where he was going to come up and I just saw this arm flapping on the surface. He couldn't get his head up and then he broke the surface with this "WHHHHH0O0O0O0OAAAAAAARRRRRR!!" It was the most radical noise I'd ever heard. I paddled straight in toward him and started yelling "Oi" over and over to the other guys out the back to come and help. When I got to him he could hardly keep his face and mouth out of the water. I grabbed him on the back and pulled him up and his head just rolled toward me. It was gross, it had this ginormous hole in it, like, I'm talking a hole into his head where you can see through his skull. I thought he was gonna die right there in my arms. Then he kinda came to and looked at me going, "Help. Help me." It was rank. I was frozen but he couldn't move so I grabbed his board and I was, like, "Grab onto your board" but he couldn't grab anything. Nothing was working. He was trying to grab his board but even his hands weren't working. I put the board under him and he had this look in his eyes and he goes, "Ohh f**k". I didn't know how I was ever going to get him in but the other guys had gotten to us and helped me. We got him onto his board. I climbed up and held him on his board and everyone pushed us in. Heavy thing is, Mufflers has got a rip that pulls you back out away from the beach and we were fighting that. Everyone ran down to the water, got him up onto the reef. It was just so fricken intense. I didn't even really think about a neck injury because I thought the dire scenario was this massive hole in his head. The cut in his head was no big issue at all — he'd broken his neck. And he never surfed again. He's in a wheelchair. But what a legend. His name's Grant Boxall, he's now the crazy Olympian and plays wheelchair rugby. My dad had it all on film but erased it all. It was gross. It was too heavy. Way too heavy to keep.

TB TIP

CARRYING YOUR BOARD. This is pretty much about looks and not function. The most accepted way is nose forward, bottom of the board toward against you. There's no real advantages or disadvantages either way except if you have the deck toward you, you'll rub wax onto your clothes or wetsuit.

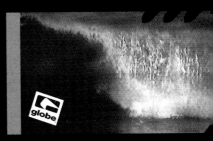

01 02 03

SEQUENCE: TWIGGY

A

A. CHOPPITIES. LEARN THESE AND YOU'LL ALWAYS HAVE SOMETHING UP YOUR SLEEVE AT THE END OF AN ORDINARY, BUMPY WAVE. B. HUH? WHY THE GRIM FACE? TB HAD TO BRING HIS BOARD INTO THE PARK FOR FEAR OF IT BEING RACKED FROM HIS VEHICLE. TAKE TAKE NO RISKS WITH THE GOLD.

CHOP HOP

CHEESE WHIZ OR 180 AIR-TO-SPIN [PG // 123]

DESPISED BY THOSE OLDER KIDS WHO REGARD ANY MANEUVER ABOVE THE LIP AS A CRIME AGAINST THE PURITY OF SURFING. BUT PROBABLY LOVED BY YOU, YOUR MATES AND EVERY OTHER FREE-THINKING INDIVIDUAL.

Chop hops pull chicks. What's a rail turn to chicks on the beach? Nuthin! What's a little air-spin then? It's fun, it's the bluff for exceptional surfing talent and it looks like you've got your s**t going on.

INSTANT RELEASE...

▶ There are three types of chop hops: the backside choppity, the out-on-the-flats choppity and the frontside on-the-face choppity. While they're poor man's airs, I reckon they're an essential skill that must be learned. They are, afterall, the first step toward you getting some real altitude.

▶ A backside chop hop with wind blowing into the face is the best way to induct you into the chop hop club. They're easiest when there's a little bump in the face, but the bump isn't essential. You'll learn later that chop-hops on the sucky part of the wave are the easiest way to feign airs but for now, just get the feel on flatter water.

▶ You might be able to ollie a two-and-a-half-foot bit of timber with wheels but you've got to ollie a six-foot piece of foam here and it's tougher. Or is it? You're not actually slamming back the tail, dragging the front foot up the deck, which lifts the tail in skating.

▶ Way it works in our hood is you're using your the rail on your toeside. That's why it's far easier to spin than to do an ollie and keep going straight. Okay, you ready?

▶ With moderate speed, roughly aim the nose of your board at the beach. Before you start, do a really slight fade to your heelside rail. This creates a tiny ramp to pivot from. In a really quick

motion, plant weight on your back foot (with a little more pressure on your toes). A microsecond later, hit the power supply on your front foot, most of the weight on your toes. This rail will lift you from the water along with the wind. At the same time, lift your arms to 'pop' you out of the water.

▶ Where to now? Look toward that wash on your inside rail. Where you look is where you go and you gotta spin that thing around. Chances are, you'll land and flick out (that's if you got air!) because your feet will be weighted toward that toeside rail.

▶ If all goes well, you will have landed halfway around, tail to the beach. Now, the important part: spin ya head! Spin it! Over the shoulder! Look over your shoulder and to the beach! This will complete the 360 motion. You're done! You've done a cheese whiz aka the chop hop.

▶ When trying them on your forehand, point your nose to the beach at, say, 45 degrees, and pop it! When you've done that, hunt 'em on the flats when a wave closes out.

▶ A few rules: they can be rank so don't take em to pointbreaks, unless right on the dying stages of the wave. Don't try 'em on perfect waves. Don't try em at the start of waves. This is the turn for making s***ty waves fun.

▶ Once you get confident on your backside you can try them off the lip or on closeouts. Do one on your frontside off the lip and you've got yourself an alley oop!

TB TIP

BEAUTY IS IN THE EYE OF THE BEHOLDER. One man's gold is another's teak. Think about how differently everyone surfs: some surf off the front foot, others off the back. Some guys are fat, some are slim. It's no wonder some people hate boards while others love them. It happens all the time with my boy Stamos. I have a board that I don't think I like and I lend it to him (well, pretty much give it to him) and he just flares up on it. AND THEN I WANT IT BACK! And then a couple of times I have got it back and it still sucks. Then there's crazy boards we both think are epic. Those boards are joy.

WHIPPING IN

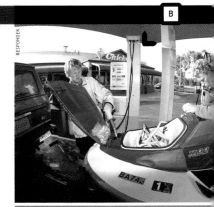

WHEN YOU MIX A TON OF METAL WITH 1200 HORSEPOWER, YOU'VE GOTTA EXPECT SOME SERIOUS LICKINGS. I'LL TALK ABOUT THE JOYS OF GETTING WHIPPED IN SOON BUT, RIGHT NOW, I GOTTA TELL YOU ABOUT HOW NAILED MY DAD GOT. I'VE SEEN THOSE GNARLY JETSKI MOVIES WITH ALL THE WIPEOUTS, BUT MY DAD'S TOASTING SMASHED THOSE THINGS.

He did the stupidest thing I've ever seen. He was getting all cocky, not towing anyone, just fanging across the face of this six footer. The wave started to bottom out and I'm on the beach going, "He'd want to pull off soon" but he kept fanging at top speed. Then, he tried to straighten out and the wave bottomed out so hard that the thing nose dived! The ski nose dived into the sand bank! The tail kicked up and my old boy went head over the hangers! Both the lip and the ski hit him. Physically, he was fine but mentally he was so rattled. It was evil.

Laird Hamilton and Darrick Doerner started the ski craze in Hawaii. They started towing with Zodiacs before progressing to skis.

My shaper at the time, Maurice Cole, got me into tows. And being the kind of classic dude he is, of course he had a ski he wanted to sell. He talked Jake Paterson and I into it and we threw down 11 gees. Eleven grand for a piece of s**t. It was a good ski but it had been flogged.

Anyway, it's tough to explain when you haven't whipped or been whipped so this tip's kinda broad.

HOW TO BE TOWED...

▶ You've got to do it when there's no one around. It's so dangerous it's surprising no one's been killed yet.

▶ When you get picked up, you don't lay, then kneel then stand. You've got to stand on your board, give the driver the okay, then be ready for the squirt of juice. You'll butcher it at the start but you'll get it. Trust me.

▶ You're at the whim of the driver. What the driver does, you do. Your legs will never know so much pain.

▶ So, be cool. Never let go when you're right on a section. Let go early and try to lose a little speed first, or you'll be going too fast to do anything. Don't try to get real high, you'll just flick out. Mess with carves.

▶ Keep your arms ready for whiplash if your driver's a bit erratic.

How to tow...

▶ Keep your eye on the ocean and look for darker swells. They're usually the sets.

▶ Steer clear of the rope because it will destroy your beast if it gets caught in the motor. And make sure it's clear of the surfer when you take off. It's unbelievably easy to get your man tangled up. Try to outrun a set and you could strangle your boy.

▶ You need to be out of the wave before it's even close to breaking. The biggest misconception is that you need to whip around the line-up really fast when you've got someone on the back. All you need is enough speed so your surfer doesn't drop into the water.

▶ Pick your swell. It usually doesn't matter what size the wave is – most of the time you're only trying to punt and can do that on a half-a-foot wave. Cruise onto the wave before it breaks. Get the ski over the back of the wave and keep on top of or over the back of the wave and stay there. Don't wreck the face. As the surfer's approaching the section, give the throttle a little squirt.

▶ There's so many options to whip into big waves. Say you're surfing a big right like Margaret River Bombie. You can be driving back into the lineup when a wave pops up. You can motor toward the section, then kick a left or right turn to whip the guy into the peak. (You know, those big hack photos you see?) By kicking a left turn you're out of the way. By whipping a right turn, the surfer will get a better pulse of power BUT... you're on the wave. No big deal, you shouldn't actually be that close to the peak and you can easily outrun anything on a good ski.

▶ There are so many options. You can whip from behind, ride down the face. Whipping takes lots of practise but is dangerous as all hell. Like I said, pretty soon they'll be taking a ski rider from the beach with a sheet over him.

TB TIP

GETTING WAVES IN A CROWDED LINE-UP. If you're on a pointbreak, try to find yourself your own little area. What I mean is this, if you're on the end of one section and away from the last guy in line you'll be ahead of the next crew and you'll be able to get the waves they can't get onto. By sitting in the pack, if you can catch it, so can they.

A. SEE, A WAVE ON YOUR OWN. B. TB FILLS THE SKI AND BEST FRIEND STAMOS EXAMINES THE TOW-ROPE WHILE THE SPECTER OF FAST FOOD LURKS IN THE BACKGROUND. C. STAMOS AND TB. D. SKI PUNTS WILL PUT A SMILE ON YOUR FACE. LIKE, COULD HIT-TING A SECTION AT 30 CLICKS AND JAMMING SOME ALMIGHTY CUTBACK OR PUTTING YOURSELF INTO ORBIT (LIKE TB ON THE RIGHT) BE ANYTHING BUT THE BEST FUN OF YOUR LIFE?

ADVANCED FLOATERS

AS YOU BECOME MORE EXPERIENCED WITH FLOATERS, BOTH BACKSIDE AND FRONTSIDE, YOU'LL TAKE CONTROL OF WHAT GOES DOWN UP ON THE LIP. YOU'LL KNOW WHEN TO USE THEM FOR FUNCTION (GETTING AROUND A SECTION) OR WHEN TO USE THEM AS AN IMPRESSIVE TRICK. HERE'S HOW TO MIX UP YOUR FLOATERS.

Floaters on sucky waves rule because falling off a genuine lip is dangerous, weightless and stylish. It's a drop into the unknown with wash exploding around you as you land. Can they get better? Dude, you know they can. From here you can do a taildrop floater or even a 360 floater.

THE TURN OR THE DROP?

▶ Okay, so you've worked out how long you can stay up there and you've been pushing it and landing some critical floaters. Good. To make a taildrop floater, you'll need a slightly more forgiving section so start your drop a second earlier.

▶ Here's another thing you've learned that you now should forget. When you're over the lip, don't turn your board towards the beach. The moment you do, a taildrop is right out of the question. To do this move, you've gotta put weight on your front foot. If you've

turned your nose, it will go down first and you will nosedive or, at best, make the move look rank. So how do you do it? Lean forward, feel the lip take your tail away from you, extend your back leg and wait for your fins to take hold. Feel your weight reconnect with the board and the speed come back into it. Yeeoooww, you're ready for the next move!

▶ Attempt a lot of floaters. If it's offshore, try a floater every wave and learn how the wave folds and when you should get out. Always look to the bottom of the wave when you're on the lip. This will help you get out clean.

Get me outta here

▶ When it's really late, the sirens are ringing and you've got to get off the lip, you can do the lunge-jump. This is when you haven't gotten off the lip before the trough and you're trying to ride over it before the wave implodes. No taildrop here, you've got to turn off the lip and almost jump your way clear to safety.

▶ The aim is to land and be slightly cushioned by the wave when it breaks after landing on the flats. Keep your arms by your side and try to be light and ready for the impact.

The wiggle

▶ This will be the only time I'll encourage you to wiggle. When you're on the lip you're riding on aerated foam so your board is easy to wiggle. Use your weightlessness to wiggle the board up again after you've started your descent. It throws another little bit of spray and makes the floater look totally involved. You've just put in a move where there

shouldn't have been one. Cool, huh?

The frontside 360 floater

▶ This move is rare. I rarely do one but it's still a cool move to have in the arsenal. The hardest thing about a floater 360 is that it goes against all the rules because you can't see where you're going. It's an extension of a taildrop, pretty much. Just remember this: your head will make you turn. Don't bother doing it with your body. Look back around your shoulder and distribute your weight evenly. Make sure there's enough weight on your back foot to make the tail drop. Lean forward when you feel it start to slide away. Keep looking to the flats, where you wanna slide down to, and let the fins break free. When they grab, be ready, or you'll be bucked. Don't try to do the full 360 in one move, just make the first 180. The rest will be easy. Keep low.

▶ The second half of the turn is easy, though maybe that's just me and I've been hanging around with pro's too long. Anyway, you can bring it back around as soon as your fins grab or you can style on backwards for a while. Depends how urgent it is that you get organized for the next section. I'll let you decide that one.

And backside 360 floaters? I've only ever seen it done once, by Hawaii's Shane Dorian in the Taylor Steele vid, *Focus*. Practice these maneuvers (reverse the above instructions) and you'll be a rare fish indeed.

tb's
BOOK OF HOT SURFING

A. TAJ (LEFT) AND ANDY (RIGHT) SPLIT A PEAK. B. SURFING IS ALL ABOUT MAKING WAVES AND DOING IT IN A WAY THAT FEELS AND LOOKS GOOD. HERE, TB GIVES UP SOME TUBE VISION FOR A ROOF RIDE.

FLARING

You may never do an air in your life. And I'll say here, you may never do an air in your life and you can still be one of the most experienced and best surfers on Earth. For me, this section is my favorite because I love airs. My dad always says to me "concentrate on basic surfing" which I should, but really, the only thing that'll help me in is contests. To tell you the truth, having won a few comps, finishing second to the world title, my whole opinion about the tour has changed. I used to really want a world title and I kinda still do, I mean I love doing the tour, but at the moment I'd rather do a huge crazy punt and stick it on front of everyone than get through a heat. And I feel the more I get loose and try not to get my three to the beach, the more popular I've become. Crazy stuff is what people remember, not who got through. I just love airs. I love the feeling of racing down the line looking for a section. I love the feeling of losing track of everything else. I love the feeling when you connect with the wash. I love it when you make a turn and stand tall in the foam. To surf a wave completely and perfectly is to do everything: throw the tail, do a huge hack, fricken everything and then do a huge punt at the end. I'm pretty sure everyone likes something from a huge hack to a huge punt. If you can do all that, it's all-time. Hopefully, these pages will help you get there...

SURF SEQUENCE: BOSKO. PORTRAIT: STEVE SHERMAN

A

MAKING AN AIR REVERSE LIKE THIS IS A REWARD FOR ALL THOSE YEARS OF THROWAWAY AIRS. WITH KNOWLEDGE, IT CAN BE A MOVE YOU PERFORM WITH SPEED, SKILL AND PRECISION.

SEQUENCE: TWIGGY

A

A. STILL LOOKS GOOD, THE OL' FRONTSIDE AIR, THE STANDARD MOVE THAT'S NOW AS COMMON AT AIRSHOWS AS A FLOATER IS AT AN ASP EVENT. THINK ABOUT IT: HOW GOOD WOULD YOU FEEL GETTING THIS HIGH, PROJECTING THIS FAR AND STICKING A LANDING THIS CLEAN AND SMOOTH. B. CARS CAN PROVIDE A SHORT ROUTE TO CRIPPLEDOM OR WORSE. LEAVE THE FAST, TIRE-BURNING CRAP TO THE KIDS IN THE 'BURBS .

FRONTSIDE AIR

SO, WHY ARE YOU HERE? WHY ARE YOU TRYING AN AIR? ARE YOU READY FOR THIS? ARE YOUR KNEES AND BOARDS READY FOR THIS?

A quick checklist before you go any further, kid:
- You've broken a board.
- You've face-planted the sand.
- You've dreamt about racing along a wave and leaving the lip.

OKAY, YOU'RE READY...

▶ Making an air is a state of mind. You might think you've made airs but it's really good there was no camera on the beach to capture the moment. Airs are difficult. They... are... so... not... easy. If you do an air within your first three years of surfing you are a freak.

▶ Sorry about the negativity but I hear guys in the lineup talking about airs they've made. These things aren't even credit card airs, they're like a tiny freefall drop from a floater.

Air reverses vs standoid airs?

▶ An air reverse is where you're trying to land on the lip with your tail then spin around in the wash. With a straight air you're trying to land your nose on the lip and glide down over the wash. I think an air reverse may be easier though. I did reverses before I did airs and I think that's the natural way to airs.

Speed or bottom turn?

▶ When you're looking at the section don't try to go as high as you possibly can. It's like when you try to really smash a golf ball. You do a way better job when you relax a little. Ease up the face — no sharp bottom turn — then launch from the edge of a spilling lip. If you come too hard off the bottom you'll get no projection 'cause you've spent your speed climbing the section. We're trying to get distance

and launch, not a vertical reo.

How much speed?

▶ It's rare that you'd ever have too much speed to go for an air.

What kind of sections?

▶ The optimum wave is one where the pulse you're on is bigger than the section you're approaching. Also, it's way easier to punt from a section that's peeling toward you rather than an entire folding section. If it's all folding you're probably better off doing a floater.

Wind?

▶ It's almost impossible to punt in an offshore wind. Punting in onshore or sideshore conditions is that much easier because you're launching into the wind, not away from it. The wind helps lift your board up (like a kite) and then keeps it near your feet. My advice? Unless you've already got airs wired, don't bother when it's offshore. Stick to floaters, hacks, cutbacks etc.

Stance?

▶ Ease up the face with a decent stance. You're going to need a foot toward the tail to get you out of the water (but not right on the tail because your bottom turn will send you too vertical). In the air your back foot then needs to move forward.

Style?

▶ Do what works. Once you've stuck an air, then assess. An air with a rank style is better than no air at all.

Grabbing?

▶ As above. If it works, it works. A standard frontside is easiest.

Monos?

▶ When your nose is higher than your

tail in the air. Again, worry about it only if you're making airs.

Commitment?

▶ Commitment is essential. Anyone can do a throwaway. Stay over your board even if it means a smaller air. Look down. Land on the lip, not on the face.

How close are you to making one?

▶ If the nose of your board is without any pressure dings or indentations, then chances are no.

TB TIP

OKAY, SO I LIKE CARS A LITTLE BIT. Despite having lost my license I'm not a crazy speed freak. I'm not like Parko and those guys trying to pump up my kilowatts and all that gear, I'm more about a good looking vehicle than something that's crazy fast. I just got a new Audi, got the kit put on but flagged the spoiler because they're too much. All I'm trying to say in a roundabout kinda way is be careful in cars. I've crashed before and it's so easy to do. A few stupid moves and you're dead. You listening? Dead. Be cool behind the wheel.

globe

SEQUENCE: RESPONDEK

A

A. DIG ON TAJ'S LEFT HAND IN SHOT ONE. IN THE FRENZIED SPLIT-SECOND OF TAKE-OFF THE HAND IS SEARCHING FOR THE RAIL. BY THE SECOND SHOT HE'S GRABBED AND IS UP AND OUT. SEQUENCE TAKEN AT ONE OF TAJ'S FAVORITE WINTER ESCAPES.
B. SHOELESS FEET ARE HAPPY FEET. HAPPY FEET ARE INSTRUMENTS OF SURFING MAYHEM.

BACKSIDE AIR

WANNA KNOW WHAT I LOVE? PULLING UP TO A BEACH AND THE WIND'S BLOWING PERFECTLY FOR BACKSIDE AIRS. IT NEVER HAPPENS IN WEST OZ SO WHEN IT DOES, OR I'M ON THE EAST COAST, I FREAK OUT.

The surf'll look so rank but I know the conditions and that I'll be able to do an air every wave. Everyone else is usually, like, "I'm over it". I'll go out and have the craziest session ever. I just put on my favorite song, like, right now it'd be this one by CKY (from the Bruce section in *Momentum Under the Influence*), suit up, throw some wax down, and get out there.

ENJOYING ONSHORES...

▶ If the wind's right, like blowing into the lefts, I'm all over it. The main difference between frontside and backside airs is what you do when you get to the lip. On your forehand it's really easy to bottom turn into it and throw yourself into and launch from the lip. Backside, you've still got to bottom turn but spring at the right time, almost like you're a fricken jack-in-the-box.

▶ If I can see a little closeout section approaching I like to stall and hang close to the peak and wait until I get enough room for two pumps before the section. The wave should be closer to sucky than fat, a little wave peeling toward you or just some kind of lip closeout that's not too dumpy.

▶ A fat, washy closeout is really tough because it's too flat to launch from.

▶ As you bottom turn up the face, your board needs to leave the wave at about a 45 degree angle. Right now, you've still got your weight on your back foot.

▶ When you reach the top of the lip you need to pop above it and put your weight to your front foot. Be confident here, you're making this thing. Look at where you want to land, know you're

going to land. When I'm in the air I like to grab my rail to steady myself, keep everything in control and keep the board under my feet.

▶ It's all front-foot weight right now until you touch the wave again. When you land on the lip you still need to ride over the wash, so keep a good solid distribution of weight across both feet. By keeping your arms in the air, you'll be able to ride over any bumps and let them take the force.

▶ When you're first learning b/s punts, don't concentrate so much on making them. Try racing toward the lip and getting in the air. Your board will probably flick out at the start but when the wind's right try them a lot. Start trying to grab when you're feeling confident. Try keeping your board under your feet the whole time. You might go weeks without an opportunity but when the wind's right, try 'em on every wave you can. Landing a good one, landing any one really, feels absolutely amazing. Just... *try*.

TB TIP

SHOE FEET. When I get off a plane and try to go straight for a surf, I just slip straight off my board 'cause my whole body's just greasy. It's heavy. In America, I don't know whether it's because the water's oily, it's the diet or whatever but my boards and my feet feel so slippery. It can wreck a late you've been hanging out for all day. If I'm going to surf in a heat I always take my shoes off at least 30 minutes to an hour before I'm meant to surf a heat just to dry 'em out. Rub your feet in the sand, rough 'em up on the rocks. I wax my feet too. It's the full old-school technique where you wax the tops of your feet and once you paddle out, you rub the top of your foot against the sole of the other. Freaky, but it works.

03

02

06

05

04

A

A. TO SIMPLIFY MATTERS, THINK OF AN ALLEY OOP AS AN AIR THAT SENDS YOU ORBITING TAIL FIRST, NOT NOSE FIRST. IT'S A MOVE DRAWN FROM SKATING, PIONEERED BY CALIFORNIANS CHRISTIAN FLETCHER AND TIM CURRAN. BEAUTIFULLY SIMPLE, ELEGANT, IMPRESSIVE. TO BE HONEST, TEEBS DOESN'T MAKE THIS ONE BUT IT'S THE PERFECT EXAMPLE OF LEAVING THE LIP. TURN THE PAGE TO SEE WHAT TO DO ONCE YOU'RE IN THE AIR.

ALLEY OOP

WHEN I WAS 13 I WENT TO CALIFORNIA AND SURFED RINCON AND EVERYONE WAS FROTHING ON THIS KID, TIM CURRAN. I WAS LIKE, "MAN, THIS GUY'S FAMOUS." THEN FOR YEARS I DIDN'T HEAR A THING ABOUT HIM. THEN I GET *MOMENTUM TWO*.

01

I'm watching and this kid I vaguely recognised raced across a left, bottom turned and did a turn I've never seen – this weird tail-first 360 air. I was like, "Nooo, that's that kid! Oh, and why didn't I think of that?" Within a few months I started to get 'em. Now they're one of my favourite manoeuvres.

OOP DOGGY...

▶ Okay, let's get one thing straight – an alley oop is not a chop hop and a chop-hop is not an alley oop. When you do an oop it's a definite bottom turn and launch off the lip. It's not like a cheap springing of your body, which a chop-hop is. In a chop hop you use your own energy to spring, but an oop you use the power of the wave to launch off the lip.

▶ So, what is an alley oop? It's a 360 air off the lip which you can only do on your forehand. I guess if you do it on your backhand, it's a Gorkin flip. And an alley oop isn't a 360 air. Just recently I've been getting really close to pulling a frontside flip which has an entirely different set of principles too. (Read about that on page 160.)

▶ Like most air-type deals, wind plays an important role. You'll see the wind's direction in this sequence. That's the best wind for it. Anything onshore will do.

▶ The wind's onshore, now you're looking for the right section. It's easier to do alley oops at the end of a peeling wave than on a closeout. You can do them on closeouts but they make for a rough landing.

▶ I do alley oops when it's a peeling wave because you don't get a direct section coming at you. You're looking for a lip that you can't get under to hit. I bottom turn right next to the lip, fly straight up, and push off my inside rail.

▶ Find the right section. The one pictured is a good because the wave isn't too steep to land on but is steep enough to get some pop out of the lip.

▶ Two major factors now. You are not trying to do a 360 and you are not trying to go high. You'll notice my tail leaves the water and my tail enters the water. If you try to do the 360 motion off the lip, you'll end up on the back of the wave.

▶ You should bottom turn up the face at around 70 degrees. When you get to the top you need to pop off the lip. A pop is just a really quick jab of power through the front of your feet. Throw your arms up at this point. All you have to do is get your board out of the water. Extending your legs (they're reasonably crouched moving up the face) will give you more height. But we're after technique, not height alright? Using this technique, you should get out of the water.

▶ After you've practised getting air you have to start making them. When you're in the air, the wind does all the work, so you have to go with it. Keep your front foot planted (it helps if you have a wide stance) and push your back foot toward the wind and the face.

▶ I know there's a lot to do up there but you need to look down over your inside rail. Even though you don't know it, this will make your body torque and help you land properly.

▶ Look for a little wash rather than landing out on the flats. This will save you face slaps and ankle grief. As you land you'll still be backwards and will probably still be looking down. Look at the flats in front of the spot where you launched. If you look down the wall, you won't do the 360 part.

▶ And one more thing. Some people will conquer oops but never do proper standard airs. Likewise, some kids can do airs but stink up oops. Wanna know why? Well, you're leaving the wave off a totally different rail. Oops are your inside rail, airs are your outside rail. Practise when you're kicking off waves and look over your shoulder toward the wave and you'll start to know what I'm talking about.

TB TIP

IN AND OUT. Yeah, it's all groovy getting out the back but don't forget you've got to get in. At joints like Lennox Head on the east coast of Australia it's tougher to get in than it is to get out. Tips? Watch where other people go. If it's rocky, ride on the top of the wash, not on the front. And always be ready to roll and get out.

01

04

05

A

HOW TO

BECOME A MORE WORLDLY SURFER [BY DEREK RIELLY] PG // 137

THE RULES...

1. Learn about your surfboards. The more you know, the more you listen to shapers and good surfers, the better they'll get, the better you'll surf.

2. Don't freak out on not wearing sunscreen occasionally. For all the sun's bad press, it's still good to get a little UV hit every now and again.

3. Gradually build a quiver. You'll surf better and gain confidence quicker if you ride the right boards. Too short boards in big waves are a fast track to mental anguish.

4. Soon as you turn 16, get your license. New waves, new challenges... watch your surfing level soar.

5. Don't like crowds? Get up earlier.

6. As hard as it is to accept, you don't deserve every wave that breaks. If you sense you're catching more than your share, pull back a little.

7. Get on a trip to a new country: Mexico, Fiji, wherever, as soon as you can. Develop that spirit of travel within. The best surfers are always guys who've thrown 'emselves over the ledge at all the world's radical spots.

8. Jetskis are indulgent, expensive, unreliable toys. Also, about the funnest things in the whole world.

9. Weed makes you paranoid, burns precious braincells, slows you down. It doesn't make you surf better.

10. Tahitian and Hawaiian waves are the biggest challenges you'll face as a surfer. Go there and stare 'em down.

11. Underpants are useless pieces of equipment. Roam free like the buffalo.

12. Go barefoot as much as society allows, feel the earth between your feet. Dunno what it is, but it really does make you feel grounded.

13. Most girls dig sex but 'cause we wind up calling girls-who-put-out sluts, most don't hunt their desires like us.

14. Old men hang at bars. Full stop.

15. It is *so* easy to die in a car crash even without a neckful of liquor. Be careful out there.

16. Nightclubs are great fun except when you wake up at 11 and drums are going off in your head and you missed the early morning offshore.

17. Know why you do reos and cutbacks and place 'em on the wave accordingly.

18. No music is cool or uncool. If it works it works.

19. MP3 is the future.

20. You can be the world's best gamer on your XBox or PS2 but if you can't make a clean waft or land an air or at least paddle out on a good day your life is a long way from being truly satisfying.

TB TIP

SWIMMING. If you asked Koby Abberton what was good training for surfing, he'd have you in the gym pumping iron. But, for me, there's nothing better for surfing than surfing. If you really want to push it, then ocean swimming's the go. The more you're in the rough water with your head down and dealing with the mental anguish of surviving without air, the more confident you'll be in the water.

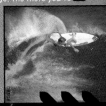

01

03

04

A

A. TB AND AN ALMOST DOUBLE GRAB. YOU COULD CALL THIS A LIEN AIR IF YOU WANT TO GET ALL SKATE TECH. B. TAHITI, WAVE OF THE DAY, CHOKING LIKE A SMALL DOG EATING A BIG BONE.

AIR GRABS

I DON'T REALLY MIX IT UP WITH GRABS THAT MUCH. MOST HAVE COME FROM SKATING AND WHAT THEY'RE THROWING AROUND IS MILES FROM WHAT WE HAVE TO DEAL WITH. LIKE, A MOVING HUNK OF WATER AND SIX FEET OF FIBERGLASS.

I mean, you can grab if it gets you hot but plenty look and feel awkward. I like my standard airs: the double grab, the normal frontside grab and the Indy.

This past week I've been surfing on the mid-north coast of New South Wales filming with Jack McCoy for Andy Irons' new vid *Blue Horizon*. It's strange. I normally do at least one air a session. The waves we were surfing were fun and usually I'd be punting like mad. This time I was racing along the waves, thinking about what tricky stuff I could get going on, but I couldn't make a thing. I'd be spending time on carves and hacks and then I'd go for airs and I wasn't over my board enough and everything felt weird.

Every now and again I go through stages like that. So I went back to basics. Back to the good ol' double grab. It's the easiest and most reliable grab and after that I was cool.

The only thing not on this page is the double grab, which is pretty obvious, and the Superman. It feels so surreal to be flying through the air with your legs kicked out. But it happens way quicker than what you think. You don't get as much time in the air as a dirtbike rider or a BMX guy so you just quickly kick your legs out and try and get the board back under your feet in time. In theory it's simple, but it really is complicated. The best thing is to try 'em off the back of the wave and practice landing back on your board.

Here are the rest of the grabs so you know what they're all about. Music...

REGULAR FRONTSIDE

Lien / Slob Crail / Melancholy Stalefish / Mute Frontside

REGULAR BACKSIDE

Method (only if tweaked) / Slob Crail / Backside stalefish / Mute Indy

GOOFY FRONTSIDE

Slob Crail / Lien / Mute Frontside / Melancholy Stalefish

GOOFY BACKSIDE

Backside crail / Slob / Method / Mute Indy / Backside stalefish

☐ Grab with front arm
■ Grab with back arm

TB TIP

CHOKING. You've waited so long for a wave, you get the bomb of the day and everyone is hooting. You've made thousands of waves yet why now — with all of these people staring at you – are you feeling a little shaky? Just like looking up too early when hitting a ball, you've got to take one thing at a time. Slow it down. Paddle hard, look at the bottom of the wave and not the wall, ride out the drop and take it one turn at a time. Get confidence from the crowd and rise to performance levels you never knew you had. If there's hardly any waves and all of a sudden a bomb comes, it's hard to step it up.

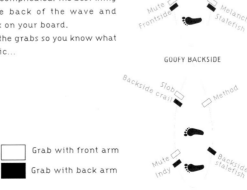

SEQUENCE: RESPONDEK.

A

A. SIX CLONED TBS SHOW EACH MOTION OF THE FRONTSIDE AIR REVERSE. NOTE THE WEIGHT ON THE FRONT FOOT TO KEEP THE FINS OUT OF THE WATER. B. THESE WOMEN AWAIT.

FRONTSIDE AIR REVERSE

AT THE START OF 2002, I DID A TRIP TO TAHITI WITH *SURFING* MAGAZINE. IT WAS LIKE THEIR SUPERTRIP OR SOMETHING. IT WAS ALL US YOUNGER GIBLETS FROTHING AROUND FOR 10 DAYS. Y'KNOW, CJ HOBGOOD, JOEL PARKINSON, MICK FANNING, ANDY IRONS AND CORY LOPEZ.

There's two reasons I'm talking 'bout this and I'm not trying to oops it up. The first is going from scarier waves to fun little rippable things and the push you get from surfing with guys who push you. So we'd been surfing Chopes and there'd been a few evil things out there and and we went to this really rippable little right. I was frothing to flare up and I probably wouldn't have done any good airs if I was just surfing by myself. Having all those guys out there made everyone get psyched up. It's kinda weird because we all thought we weren't surfing that good because we all had such high expectations of ourselves. Everyone wants to surf their very best in front of their friends. Whenever I did something minor, I was like, "God, I'm stinking it up. I'm having a shocker." Then we went back and watched the footage, and we were all saying, "Oh, there were a few keepers." When everyone's there you just want to surf really good. It's hard to explain. The funny thing is that it wasn't that good a session. Everyone was over it. It wasn't the most memorable session or anything.

BACK IT UP...

▶ You need speed. And you need to find a good section. Initially, closeouts are the go because they give you broken water to land on. As you know, closeouts aren't always easy to punt on, so you need to work out what suits you. For me, the best section is a soft wash with a throwing lip at the top.

▶ Hit the lip too early and you'll go off the back. Hit it too late and you'll be back-slammed and wear a lip to the head.

▶ Widen your stance as you bottom turn because it's way easier to stay in control. Put your front foot a little further forward than normal and your back foot right on the tail. Don't put too much power into the bottom turn otherwise you won't have enough speed to punt. Also, try to stay relaxed. If you try to go huge, you'll probably just flick your board out.

▶ So as you bottom turn and look at the lip, think about going beyond it. You're trying to ollie/jump off the lip.

▶ Before you leave the lip, you've probably brought your board up at a 45-degree angle. You need to follow your tail through at that same angle.

▶ I find air reverses easier. When I hit I like to push with my back foot and the board spins easily. Once in the air, I like to grab my rails. Some people find this tough but if you've got a low center of gravity, it's where your hands will naturally go.

▶ Wind is crucial. Making airs in an offshore wind is almost impossible. If the wind is onshore it's perfect for airs, same if the wind is blowing the opposite way to where you're headed.

▶ Landing. Be committed. Know where to land and know you're going to make it – half of it's in your mind. Try to land on the wash and not in the trough or out on the flats. Always look where you're going to land. Keep your weight on your front foot. If it's on your tail, you'll dig in and bog.

▶ It's hard to explain how to do these things on paper but getting up there is the key. Once you get off the wave, you'll be able to realize what I'm talking about. You might try 100 of these and make none. The day you stick one, it'll all be worth it.

TB TIP

WANNA GET MORE PLAY? I'm no expert in romance but I know this, once you approach a girl (or a member of the opposite sex) and are stuck for idle chit-chat, don't talk about yourself. Please. Ask questions, show interest and listen to the answers. If you ask vital questions twice, you're out. And don't wait till you're necked to make your move. The kid who did it sober is the one who gets the prize.

globe

BACKSIDE AIR REVERSE

SURFING'S A WEIRD GAME. THERE'S NO TEXTBOOK WAY OF DOING THINGS. IF IT WORKS, IT WORKS. BUT YOU CAN'T JUST STAND UP, TWIST YOUR HIPS AND WAVE YOUR ARMS IN SPONTANEOUS GUSTS AND EXPECT MAGIC TO HAPPEN. HERE'S SOME OF THE WAYS I GET MY AIRS REVERSED...

01

03

05

The backside air reverse is a strange one because it's so close to a backside air. Or is it? Ah ha! It's not, actually. It's more like a chop hop than a backside air. In fact, that's all it is: a dirty, well-placed and well-timed choppity. If you compare this sequence to the one back on page 122, you'll see the similarity once I'm the air.

SPOT THE DIFFERENCE...

▶ You have to maintain your speed up the face.

▶ You have to negotiate where you leave the wave and be careful you're not destroyed by the lip.

▶ And, finally, once you're up there,

you have to negotiate your landing, whether on the wash or on the clean green.

Leaving the wave.

▶ So, you're racing down the line and you need a section. You're looking for a wave with a bit of suck. No love on a flat face. You need suck, lift and you're going to have to push it.

▶ When you find your sucky section, move into confident mode. Spread your legs, move your toes into the wax and grip. This section's yours and you own it.

▶ When you reach the top of the wave, you actually have to do a little jump. The best thing to do is to look toward your inside shoulder as you pivot from the water.

How you can throw it into reverse.

▶ The pivotal moment in backside air reverses is that sharp snap of the head and torso when it matters. Without it you're going to fall off the back of the wave.

▶ You have to do your body snap when your tail is the last thing in the water. At the risk of pointing out the obvious, you are not a jetski. You are the engine. At some point you have to tell your board it's time to leave the water. And the time is... now!

▶ Before you're confident at leaving a lip like I am on this closeout, you can do a bluff backside air reverse. Leave the face just before the section. You're still landing on the section but you're launching on a part of the wave you're familiar with. You know it's a chop hop, others don't. This is one for the ladies.

Ready for the spin.

▶ You'll spin without realizing. And when you're in the air there's not much you can do. That's why the big stance helps because if there's a wind blowing (you'll need it to be coming toward you), spreading your hooves will hold the board to your feet.

Landing backwards.

▶ Even though you probably won't spin a full 180 degrees, you should land tail first. Your momentum will spin you around.

▶ Landing is the hardest part because when you're in the air you have no idea where you are. Look at me in the big shot. Lost in space. But because of the sizey stance I'm sporting I'm in a decent amount of control.

▶ Landing is where you'll fall most. You're spinning and reconnecting and typically your board will flick out when you make contact. The trick is to be solid and confident and trick your mind into believing you're infallible.

▶ When you land you need to keep weight on your back foot yet quickly spread it to your front foot so you spin in an even motion. Looking back to the beach will bring you 'round.

▶ Once you start to spin it's all about the weight on the front foot and a low center of gravity to ride out the bad ol bumps.

▶ You're done. If you're still standing after all that, you're good. Real good. Nice one. Now try landing one full rotation, nose pointing to the beach. If you pull one, call me. I'm under "B" in the Margaret River white pages.

06

07

09

globe

B

A. AND USE A NAPKIN. EASY. B. B/S AIR REVERSE AT A PUNTER'S PARADISE SOUTH OF NEWCASTLE ON NSW'S CENTRAL COAST. CHECK IN SHOT THREE HOW FAR TB'S LEGS ARE SPREAD. A LESSER MAN WOULD RUPTURE HIS SCROTUM PERFORMING SUCH A MOVE.

TWIGGY

A

VALUE OF A QUIVER

ONLY RECENTLY HAVE I REALISED HOW AMAZING IT IS TO RIDE A VARIETY OF BOARDS. AND THE SLIGHTEST CHANGE – JUST ONE OR TWO EXTRA INCHES IN LENGTH, OR EVEN SIXTEENTHS OF AN INCH IN THICKNESS – CAN SMOOTH YOU OUT, DRAW YOUR SURFING OUT INTO LONGER, MORE POWERFUL LINES. YOU CAN CARVE, INSTEAD OF JUST HACK.

I used to be the full-on 5'11" warrior. The surf could be anywhere from one to six foot, and I'd be out there on my trusty 5'11". Lately, though, I've been overpowering shorter boards in any waves bigger than three feet. They can hold in, but feel a bit skatey. I just can't push them as much as I want.

Check out the story on page 150 if you don't think quivers are important. You can't surf big waves without 'em. Being undergunned can be very dangerous to your health.

I feel really passionate about the value of a quiver. A quiver starts with two boards. I'm gonna tell you why they help your surfing.

BOARD BY BOARD...

▶ Watch any good surfer. He or she can jump on a surfboard and ride it well, no matter its size. Ride the one board all the time and the moment it goes away, you're probably useless. Every board will have something about it you can learn from.

▶ Remember the bumbat I rode in *Sabotaj* and did the spins and chop hops? That board helped my surfing so much. It was so easy to go backwards on it that I became relaxed with the feeling. When I got back on my normal board and found myself backwards after an air or whatever, I found I could make it almost every time.

▶ You don't have to be a big-wave legend to have a quiver. Big boards are perfect if it's five or six foot and there's a strong offshore, making it easier to get into waves. The extra volume will also make you a better duckdiver.

▶ Different boards, especially bigger boards, are amazing for fine-tuning your style. Say you're jittery between turns. A bigger board will make you do drivier turns because, well, you just can't jiggle a big board. And when the swell drops and you jump back on a smaller board, it will feel amazing. You will probably never have felt so much control over it.

▶ Whoever you are and whatever you ride, you can still break a board. It's kinda stupid to think that if you've got one board – and just one board can seriously sting your coin supplies – that everything will be alright. Boards get dinged and broken easily and you've got to get these things fixed as soon as they happen. The result? You're singing the no-board blues while they're under the knife. Have a backup or two.

▶ Riding different boards in tiny waves is also really good for your surfing. If you've got a good all-rounder, chances are it'll be sluggish in smaller waves. A different board (either bigger or smaller) can enable you to grab more speed in small waves, because it may have a wider tail and glide through dead sections.

▶ If you've got a quiver for bigger surf, then you know how good it feels to pull out a gun and paddle out on it. You feel like a true waterman if you've got a bigger board for bigger surf. You're at a massive advantage if the waves are six foot or above because you're equipped. Unlike the guys out there on their shortboards getting licked because they can't make sections,

you can lay into a serious bottom turn and set up a move way down the line. Also, in bigger surf there's more rips and currents. You need length to paddle against them, and to get out of trouble.

▶ You don't need a brand-new quiver of bigger boards, you don't even need to be pedantic about dimensions. Look around in surf shops. Guns are typically in good nick because they're ridden so rarely, which means you can buy them secondhand dirt-cheap. And once you have it, it'll last you a few years.

TB TIP

THE HOOPS OR THE WRAP? There are three main ways of dealing with your leash after a surf. There's the board wrap: two loose loops of the board in front of where you hold it. There's the old-school wrap: around the two front fins and sticking it tight with leash around the fin; or there's the loose spool: a series of neat ringlets that hang from your hand. This is the most widely used method. Or, a morphing of all.

GRABRAIL TURNS

GRABRAIL TURNS ARE RARE. YOU COULD GO FOR 20 SURFS AND NOT THROW DOWN A GRABRAIL HACK. SO, WHAT ARE THEY? HOW ARE THEY DIFFERENT TO THE NORMAL CUTBACK, THE ROUNDHOUSE CUTBACK OR THE HACK? THEY'RE BASICALLY A CUT-DOWN.

POWER IN THE FIST...

▶ Okay, there are only three times I even think about doing grabrail turns: When I'm going really fast. When the section I'm on is steep. And when I don't want to hit the wash when I'm doing a hack or cutback.

▶ Like I said before, the grabrail is a really more of a cutdown than a cutback. Most of you already know that your board will flick out and you'll fall on your back if you try to lay down a big speed carve on a sucky section. Why? Because you just can't get your rail in the water. The secret to good carving is setting your rail in the face and driving. When you're going fast on a sucky section it's too hard to both pivot and set your line at the same time.

▶ Grabrail turns feel really solid. Think about it. You've got the security of your rail, you're moving fast and the motion of grabbing enables you to control where you're headed. Look at the sequence to the right. Even if I wanted to hit the wash, the security blanket that is the rail is stopping me. All the things you know, like looking at the wash or pointing to it don't work here. Because you're right over your board, those motions would mean you'd pivot then topple over your outside rail.

▶ You can do the grabrail turn on your backhand too. On your backhand it's more about looks because it's easier to set your rail. Grabrail isn't so important because your inside hand can control you on the face even when it's sucky. Dave Rastovich does some crazy grabrails because he's got the full vogue style and has got one of those low centres of gravity. Looks hot. And I'm not talking about the kid's rig.

▶ The best grabrail turn I've ever seen was by a kid from Yamba in Australia, Dan Ross, in the surf vid *Channel One*.

He was on this punchy wedge and laid down the quickest hack I've ever seen. His turn is the perfect example of why we grab the rail. If he tried that turn without grabbing the rail, he'd be toast.

Some rules:

1. Start it early. You can't grab your rail mid turn. It's all about changing direction fast and you need to start it before your turn at the top of the wave.

2. You can't do them on a fat section. Imagine how rank your style is if you're doing a slow cutback on a fat wave.

3. By halfway down the wave, your arm doesn't really need to be there. You grab your rail to set your line and change direction. Once you've done that, you're cool.

4. Always look down to where you want to go.

5. If you aim too far above the lip, your fins will break free and you'll spin out of control. This sequence here is about as high as you should go.

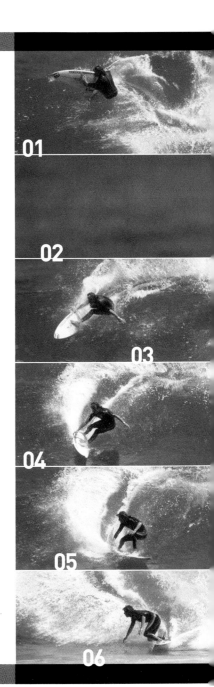

01
02
03
04
05
06

this is carpark, one of my favourite local breaks.
board was average until i sprayed it red.

grabbing rail just for the shot.

$5'11 \times 17\frac{3}{4} \times 2\frac{1}{8}$

one of the fifty i have
downstairs in my boardroom.

grab rail cutdown

↖ four fingers.

massive fin
↖ .throw

i like photo's when you can
see the tail.

into

board was average until i sprayed it red.

grabbing rail just for the shot.

one of the fifty i have

four fingers →

i like photos when you can
see the tail.

A. TEEBS AND HIS BEST FILM OF THE YEAR ACCEPTANCE SPEECH FOR *MONTAJ* AT THE *SURFER* POLL AWARDS. POPULARISED BY SIX-TIME WORLD CHAMP KELLY SLATER YEARS AGO AT JEFFREYS BAY, SOUTH AFRICA, THE GRAB-RAIL TURN IS NOW SECOND NATURE TO ALL TOP SURFERS.

B

SEQUENCE: TUNGSTEN/ZINGIN

A

A. THE MAGIC OF THIS SEQUENCE IS ALL IN THE THIRD FRAME. FULL OF CONFIDENCE, TB'S HUNG OFF THE TAIL, SOMEHOW LANDED, THEN LINED UP THE TUBE AS THE LIP EXPLODES AROUND HIM. TOUGHER THAN IT LOOKS.
B. WOULD YOU BUY A BOARD FROM THIS LITTLE MAN?

LATE DROPS

AND DEALING WITH DIFFERENT TUBES PG // 149

YOU MIGHT HAVE READ ABOUT MY OLD BOY'S SMOKING ON THE SKI BACK ON PAGE 124? WELL, HE'S NOT THE ONLY THE ONE WHO'S BEEN TOASTED...

At the start of 2003 I was on the Gold Coast. I love cyclone season up there. It's warm, there's waves, there's a casino and plenty of girls. The whole buzz of the place sets me off.

For those of you who've never experienced the Goldie, I'll paint you a picture. The place has three of the world's best pointbreaks, the mood's laid back and it seems as if everyone takes advantage of Australia's hospitable social security program. The crowds are evil.

One morning Stamos, Beau Emerton and I checked Burleigh Heads. It was four foot and there was... nobody... out! See, when the sweep's bad up there, no one can physically paddle against the rip. It's the perfect place to get the ski out. Soon we were whipping into these crazy tubes and having the best time ever. But then I whipped Stamos into a bomb and instead of squirting over the back, I hung right out in front of the pit to see him get this incredible tube. I was hooting, freaking out, but then I realized I was too late to get out of there. I crept up the wave face, the sand sucked dry and the ski's beak mowed under water and into the sand. A microsecond later and I'm tossed up over the hangers just like my old boy! I couldn't believe it! The same mistake and I'm wearing a 1200 hp ski on my head. I seriously thought I was dead, the first person to die from whipping in... and on a three foot day! It turned out I was cool but the ski was toast. The moral of the story? You need to be able to create speed when you make late drops and hit the bottom of the pit with nothing.

GET ON IN THERE, BOY..

▶ Late drops only really happen on sucky waves. On fatter waves, there usually isn't a problem.

▶ The greatest asset you'll take into the late drop is confidence. The moment your mind questions itself it's all over. The drop's late, eh? You're a good surfer, you've made thousands of drops, why is this one any different?

▶ If a ledging wave is peeling across a bank or reef don't look back into the abyss. That's not where you're taking off so don't let it rattle you.

▶ Spread your arms for balance, and use them to recoup speed after landing.

▶ Late drops go against all the physics you've learnt. Hang off your back foot when you take off and normally you're going over the falls. With late drops, if you paddle hard enough and beat the lip you can hang off your back foot and still be sweet.

▶ Drops are usually your speed run into a wave and set you up for your ride. A freefall take off like the one pictured sees you land and almost stop dead. You've got to learn to climb from the bottom without any speed. Practice it.

Okay, you're on the wave...

▶ Driving your hand, arm, shoulder in the wall is still the most efficient way of stalling. Make sure you've got a low center of gravity when you take it on otherwise you'll get smoked.

▶ Kelly's double-armed special. I've seen Kelly throw both arms in the wall to slow down. Try it without his style and the consequences could be tragic.

▶ The speed pump and the shimmy. Shimmying up your board through tubes is the best way to get out of quick pits. Wax accordingly.

▶ The doggy door. The sneaky front door exit before a wave closes out. No one can teach you when to find one, it's purely instinctive. You won't believe some of the tubes you'll make.

▶ The frontside nose or rail grab? Only use in an emergency, especially for the style kids. A bit sketchy but like I've said if it works, it works.

TB TIP

THE PRICE IS WRONG. Because I'm on a bit of a gravy train with boards, I didn't know about this one until recently. When you custom order a board and head into the factory to talk to the shaper about measurements and all that gear, it can be difficult to ask how much coin the board will sting you. Or maybe in the excitement you just forget to ask. Then you go to pick it up and are lugged with a rate far more expensive than what you assumed. Don't get burnt. Be up front, ask for the price and there'll be no untriendly surprise.

B

TWIGGY

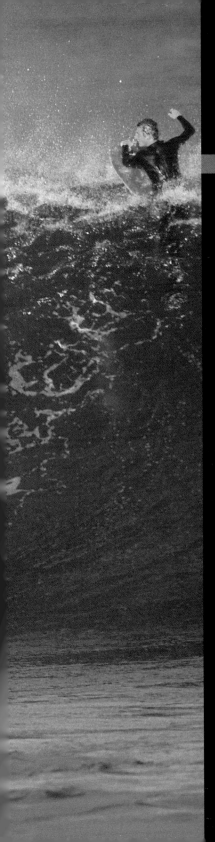

LAST YEAR TAJ'S GOOD FRIEND DAMON EASTAUGH BROKE HIS HIP AND DROVE BONE THROUGH SKIN AND RUBBER IN A WIPEOUT. TB REMEMBERS THE SESSION...

Whenever I walk up the beach with a broken board, someone always asks me if it broke from hitting the bottom. I don't think I've ever broken a board that way. Saying that, it makes you wonder how powerful waves actually are. Think about the plywood stringer of a surfboard. How much force must it take to break it on its edge? Yet even a small wave can do it. Getting caught by the lip can be worse than any belting on the bottom. Don't believe me? Read on...

August 21, 2002. I am surfing this place at home called the Womb with a mate, Damon Eastaugh. The waves are six-to-eight foot and perfect, and it's just the two of us out there. We've just paddled out and this crazy set comes through. I scream, "GO! GO!" He paddles, and everything looks sweet, but when he bottom turns he can't get up under it enough because his board is too small. He's riding a 6'3" and he's about 6'3" himself, he's huge. So he tries to bottom turn and the thing just grows above him. He sets his line for a barrel but he's too low and the thing just squashes him. So I paddle into the next one, take off, don't get barreled, go through a little section and try to straighten out when the lip comes out of nowhere and absolutely canes me. I'm underwater getting ripped around, and I'm thinking, "S**t, I wonder if he got as hammered as me."

I come up and Rictor, a photographer who'd been shooting from the water, is swimming toward Damon. I hear Damon yell, "I've broken my leg. I've broken my leg!" So I get there and he's taken off his leash because it's tugging his mangled leg. (He doesn't remember doing this and later asks me if I took it off for him.) I take off my leash and help him onto my board. He just holds on and gets washed into the sand. Rictor and I are still swimming and can see him pulling himself up the beach by his hands, dragging his legs. When we get in there, we see how mangled he is. His foot is facing the wrong way. Damon's wearing a steamer and the fricken shinbone is sticking out though his skin and his wettie. Sticking out! It's rank. We're a mile or so from the carpark and there's really thick, dark red blood pumping out onto the sand.

I'm supporting his leg, trying not to look at it. The only people around are me, Rictor and my dad, who had been shooting from the sand. I realize the three of us won't be able to get Damon back to the carpark. The sand is so soft that you sink up to your knees in some parts, and that's not carrying a dead weight. Then these bodyboarders rock up and one of them takes control, making a splint from driftwood and a leash. He ties it really tight. I can see the pain on Damon's face, and the blood is still pouring out. We lay him on the board, and start carrying him. He is the toughest dude I've ever seen. I would've freaked out but he's going, "Oh yeah, how's it look? It's gonna be alright, huh?" We keep on trucking. We have to put him down and rest about five times before we get to the car. When we finally make it, we slide him straight into the back of my wagon on his board. By the time we get to the hospital at Margarets he's shaking and freaking out. They cut open his wettie. He's busted his knee on one leg, toasted both his tibia and fibula on the other, and driven his hip out of its joint.

When I look back and see Rick's footage, the wave is so heavy. It looks like he should've been killed. And the craziest thing is, the wave did it to him, not the bottom. And how's this? When I go back a few hours later to get our gear, there's no one out, the sun's shining and the Womb is the best I've ever seen it. But I'm too rattled after what I've seen. I just pack up, turn my back and walk away. I wasn't in the mood.

A. NO UNSEEMLY CROUCH, NO PANICKED ARMS, JUST A WARM-FEELING GLIDE THROUGH THE BLUE. TB, THE WELCOME MEAT IN A HOMETOWN SANDWICH.

STYLE

OVER THE YEARS I THINK I'VE WATCHED MORE VIDEO FOOTAGE OF MYSELF THAN ANY OTHER SURFER ON EARTH. AND I RECKON IT'S HELPED ME END UP WITH THE STYLE I'VE GOT TODAY. I'M NOT SAYING I'VE GOT A PERFECT MOTION OR THAT I'M ALWAYS IN SYNC WITH THE WAVE. BUT IT'S DEFINITELY HELPED ME A LOT.

I can't remember the first time I saw myself surf on video but I know a lot of people are absolutely devastated when they do. It's like when you hear your voice recorded for the first time. You cringe because you sound so stupid. But really, we're just being harsh on ourselves.

Some people think a good style is one where your back leg's dropped nicely toward the front, your arms are by your side and everything else is aligned above your stringer. But there are no rules. Style is about personal taste. I personally love different, even awkward, approaches. Traditionally, you'd have to say Andy's style isn't perfect but I love how he looks punk and as if he doesn't care. It's the same with how wide apart my legs get when I do airs and hacks. It's different, it doesn't necessarily mean it looks ugly. Speaking of ugly, some people can't stand Cory Lopez's style, because he crouches a little and has a pretty wide stance. To me it works. Plus he's adopted his own unique maneuvers from it. Who else in the world throws out those crazy laybacks? Before you point the finger at anyone, you have to realize that for every action, there's a reaction. And I feel myself learning from everyone: pros on tour, guys who surf okay and just bust out a freak turn. You can learn something about style from every single surfer.

Good style is all about making simple turns look good. The Hobgoods do it really well on their backside reos. As they do one, they do the sweetest little tuck on the lip and it makes the turn look so good. When they get a crazy wave and use that same technique, it looks unbelievable. That's when style makes all the difference.

Besides the rush of big waves and the mental anguish of surfing them, serious surf provides the perfect environment for truly assessing someone's style. When waves are small you have a certain level of control over it. When there's fear, all thoughts of style go out the door. It's a true reflection. In big waves, you want to get from A to B... fast. With all that action going on around you, you forget about how you should look. Rob Machado is one guy who's unaffected by fear. That man was at the front of the queue when they were giving out styles.

Your environment has a lot of influence over your style too. Think about Joel Parkinson and all those years surfing the Queensland points. He's slowed it all down, smoothed it out and only turns when he has to. There's no unnecessary wiggles. He even looks like that on big waves or trashy onshore surf. The style has stuck. Then there's guys like Rasta who surf really well, but give them a down-the-line right and they come into their own. Throw him back on a left and he's just another good surfer.

Style's important to me but there are times when style is totally forgivable. If you do a crazy crazy hack or a big air, but then come out of it weird, don't turn on yourself about style. A good style's good but the moment it stops you doing turns when and where you want, let it go.

Reckon you look rank? Video, video, video. If it's a wiggle or jitter you don't dig, then ride a bigger board and see the changes that will happen to your surfing. Order new boards accordingly. And don't stylize yourself to bite someone's act. Adopt your own unique traits, steal odd moves by all means but remember there's no two surfers on earth that move the same. How good is that?

TB TIP

THE ULTIMATE SURF VID COMPILATION. There's a guy from Margarets called Scotty Lawrence who loves Kelly so much he's put together every section of Kelly from surf vids and put 'em on one video tape. Music on surf vids makes such a difference. I'm working on my third profile movie and hope to have it released by the end of 2004. I'm already hunting cool tracks. Surf vids are the greatest thing ever. There's nothing else in the world that makes you wanna surf. Like... right now!

SEQUENCE: BOSKO

A

A. HERE'S THE TB KID, WINGS PULLED BACK, RIDING A SMALL SWELL IN HAWAII, A LONG WAY FROM HIS HOME IN YALLINGUP, WA. IF YOU'RE GOING TO PUNT, THESE COLORS TASTE LIKE MUSIC. B. IT'S FIVE IN THE MORNING AND THE WORLD'S STILL SLEEPING. AND YOU'RE DOWN THERE IN THE GRIT AND GRIME CHANGING A STINKING FLAT TIRE. THIS IS THE ONE TIME OUT OF A HUNDRED YOU SHOULD'VE STAYED IN BED.

SPRAYING YOUR BOARD

SPRAYS GO IN AND OUT OF VOGUE. MISS YOUR WINDOW OF COOL AND IT'S LIKE SPORTING A VISOR WHEN TRUCKER HATS ARE THE HIPPEST THING IN TOWN. TIMING'S THE KEY. SO, WHERE TO NOW? WHAT'S THE NEXT BIG THING IN BOARD SPRAYS?

Graffiti and stenciling have been big in the past few years. I don't know how long stenciling will hold its own but for now, you can still get away with it. **Hints.**

Don't bother with a full board spray, like spraying your entire board red. It can work on guns but it makes your surfing look slow and awkward. If you had to to do it, let's say to cover a ding, a yellow spray is the most forgiving.

STENCILLING TO VICTORY...

▶ Draw or copy your image or words onto a piece of paper. Look for something obscure, whether it's words or pictures but it's best to make up your own. Failing that, trawl the net. Bizarre searches on google.com is your best friend here.

▶ Glue the paper onto a piece of cardboard around an eighth of an inch thick. Then use a scalpel to cut out your drawing from the cardboard. You now have a customized stencil.

▶ The best stencilling is when you don't get drips. Apply paint sparingly with even strokes. Tape up areas you don't want ink on with masking tape and newspapers.

Hit predictions?

My hit prediction is cammo will make a comeback. And flags. Patriotism is always a winner, especially now with the terror threats and wars, this stuff will keep rolling.

Preparation of the surface.

▶ Clean the wax and grime off your board completely.

▶ You need to rough up the board surface a little to adhere paint to the glass. Use a fine grade of sandpaper.

Designing your own boards

You've got a few options here:
- markers
- posca pens
- spray paint

▶ Spray paint smudges less than markers and poscas. Both can be cool if you use a gloss coat when you're done.

▶ Freehand spray painting is cool but you've got to be careful not to bleed and run. Try not to get too technical.

▶ Even though it's not under the glass and can be changed, the ordeal of cleaning a spray off is heavy. Be prepared for some crazy smudging and hours of frustration.

Under-the-glass sprays

No smudging, no changing minds, no worries. The under the glass spray's laid down on the board after it's shaped and before it's glassed. Because it adds a day or two to the production time of your stick, they cost more. And because you can't change your mind once you've committed, most people do it themselves.

▶ If you want a pro to do it, they can still do it on top of the glass.

▶ Pros will get cleaner lines and have the ability to airbrush and create more perfect sprays.

Biting style

There's an entire planet of ideas, so don't bite some other dude's style. If you're going to rip off a board spray, don't rip off that small group known as pro surfers. Check out design mags, go beyond the square you live in. Besides, you've probably got way better taste than your favorite pro surfer.

What else?

▶ I like tail sprays. I like the way they cut through the water.

▶ If you're getting sick of a board and it's still going good, a spray can give it a new lease of life.

▶ A good spray can make a good board feel amazing. Similarly, a spray can make a good board go bad.

TB TIP

SNOOZE. The alarm goes off and it feels like you could stay in bed forever. Seriously, no matter how bad the surf is, 99 times out of 100 you'll be glad you got up. Trust me.

B

globe

THE LIST

TAJ SPENDS NINE MONTHS OF THE YEAR ON THE ROAD, THIS IS SOME OF THE GEAR THAT GETS HIM INSPIRED...

▶ **CELEBRITY RIGS**
MILLA JOVOVICH
ANGELINA JOLIE
LAETITIA CASTA
GISELE BUNCHEN
CLAIRE MINEO
GWEN STEFANI
CAMERON DIAZ

▶ **MOVIES**
SNATCH
PULP FICTION
MEET THE PARENTS
AUSTIN POWERS (ALL)
SHAWSHANK REDEMPTION
THE BIG LEBOWSKI
PREDATOR
TRAINING DAY
ZOOLANDER

▶ **TOP TEN SURFERS**
Kelly Slater: All-time best.
Rob Machado: Always amazing to watch. Every time I see him surf I say how good he is. He always blows me away.
Andy Irons: A really fricken good punk style, and he's super determined.
Joel Parkinson: Freakish talent and draws big, drawn-out lines with that Queensland-tuned style.
Bruce Irons: I love his tuberiding and airs. Illustrated best at HT's in Indo or Backdoor and Off the Wall in Hawaii.
Shane Dorian: Has been my favorite since day one.
Hobgood brothers: They flare up and really charge.
Shaun Cansdell: A young Australian goofy-footer you should know about. Crazy, crazy natural talent.
Old Boy (Vance): Still fully flaring at figgety-three and taught me everything I know, so he reckons.

▶ **TOP SIX SURF VIDS.**
Kelly Slater in Black and White

The Blueprint
Momentum Under the Influence
Alley Oop
156 Tricks
Seven Days Seven Slaves

▶ **TOP 10 POSSESSIONS.**
G4 Powerbook
iPod
Audi A4
Commodore wagon
50 x 5'11"s
House on Yallingup Hill
My 1200 horsepower Yamaha jetski
Reclining lounge chair
Radar detector

▶ **SURF VID SECTIONS.**
Bruce Irons: Momentum Under the Influence.
Parko: Three Degrees.
Kelly Slater: Momentum II/Focus.
Dorian: Momentum II/Focus.
Ozzie: Wipeout section of 156 Tricks.
Wardo: 5'5" x 191/4"
Andy Irons: Momentum Under the Influence.
Kalani Robb: Loose Change.
Rob Machado: Momentum II.

▶ **TOP FIVE FRIENDS (NOT IN ORDER)**
1. Stamos
2. Rictor
3. Snake
4. Twiggy
5. Nathan Webster

▶ **TOP 10 WAVES**
North Pole, Western Australia: Big right reef point that is my number one fave.
Macaronis, Sumatra, Indonesia: Perfect backside pits and a ridiculously smashable wall.
Gnaraloo, West Australia: Big, slabbing, triple-ledged out long left.
Hare Mountain, Western Australia. A beachie that really pumps every now and again.
Jeffreys Bay, South Africa: So much fun flying along the wave and drawing the lines

you need to make each section.
Snapper Rocks, Gold Coast, Queensland: Always that crazy bank thanks to the Gold Coast City Council and its sand-pumping program. So much fun onshore and offshore.
Lower Trestles, California, USA: The most rippable wave ever. Light, glassy Californian winds and a slower wave speed makes you feel invincible. It's so hard to fall off.
Supertubes, Western Australia: A sick little reef at home. Tubes when it's offshore and punts when the wind swings onshore.
Mundaka, Spain: Had it perfect once and couldn't believe my eyes.

TB TIP

KEY STASHING SPOTS. Hopefully my car doesn't get racked after this little piece but here we go. All cars are different obviously, but here's a few winning spots. On the coil on the back wheels, up under the front bumper bar. Remember, if the scum want your car they'll get into anyway they want but key pockets in wetties and leashes are good too. Keys in a towel on the beach is also a safe one and at least in Oz, a legit call for insurance if your car is racked.

02

05

A

B

FRAME GRABS COURTESY OF: FRAMELINES.

A. FEELS REAL NICE TO ROUND OFF THE BOTTOM, LUNGE AT THE LIP AND RIDE OVER THE FOAM LIKE THIS. B. SHERM AND TEEBS SAVE THE CROOK FRAME GRAB-COLORED PAGE WITH A MINCY LIFESTYLE SHOT.
C. APART AND GOOD TO GO.

CARVING 360

THESE ARE EASIER THAN YOU THINK, THOUGH IT'S PRETTY RARE TO SEE 'EM OUT IN THE FIELD. LEARN 'EM, REFINE 'EM, AND YOU'LL HAVE A POWERFUL TRICK IN YOUR REPERTOIRE.

A lot of people can't do carving 360s. When I first started trying 'em, I'd just throw myself at the lip and fall forward without my board. I think they're only tough because they look so hard. You don't expect to make them in your head. But they're so much more basic than you think.

TALK TIME...

▶ The most important thing I learnt about carving 360s was from Nathan Webster. He'd done a few and was frothing out on them. His advice was that as you bottom turn, you need to cruise up the face and don't lean into it too hard. His theory was that as you head up the face, that's when you push hard through your turn. It was so easy: chill, don't squat and drive and push right at the top. After that it all started to come together.

▶ All turning is about overpowering your board and ripping it off its natural trajectory. None more obvious than the carving 360. But it's a double-pronged turn because you still have to come out of the bottom and get to the top with enough speed to jam it back around.

▶ The ultimate section is one with a washy, semi-throwing section. If it's too sucky you're going to get clipped in the head by the lip. If it's chubby, that fat old thing isn't going to be enough to kick you back down the face. You may done a 360 in the wash but this isn't a carving 360. A carving 360 happens on open face when your tail hits the lip not the nose of your board.

▶ When you're about three-fourths of the way up the face, that's when you need to break your line. A solid hit of power on the back foot will rip you into a new world.

▶ As you hit the section you need to keep a fair amount of weight on your front foot. Staying over the nose of your board is the key. It's all about coming down nose first. Again, a 360 where you come down backwards and spin once you hit the bottom isn't a carving 360.

▶ If you're falling forward without your board then you're probably motoring out of the bottom of the wave and trying to spin when you hit the lip. Your tail has to hit and you have to ride back over the foam.

▶ If you're going for carving 360s and getting close then you're skilled enough to deal with wash. Your stance in a turn like this is pretty standard. Ride it out and be ready to deal with the bumps.

▶ Once you pick it up, it's a real versatile turn. At the end of 2002, Kelly did the most freaky carving 360 at Haleiwa in Hawaii. He drove out of the bottom on what had to be a 10-foot wave and attacked this closeout. It was one of the most extraordinary things I've ever witnessed.

▶ If you're not feeling the carving three-o, studying other people's surfing is the way to go. If you've got a mate who can do the tricky gear and he's being a bit of a gatekeeper and not throwing you any tips, watch video. Fast, slow, super-slow, imprint the move into the sponge of your mind.

TB TIP

WAX ON SMOOTH. The dreaded chinese wax job. Placing your board straight on top of another without a divider is a sinister act. Regardless of the heat, the wax will melt, leaving a crook brown mess on the bottom of your craft. It also slows you down. And here's a story. Sometimes, I write my sponnos on the bottom of my boards with texta. I packed my coffin board bag, got on a flight and when I unpacked, my new craft were covered in scratches, smudged texta and wax – it was crook. Divide 'em with a towel, a wettie, whatever. Just keep those kids apart.

MORRIS

A

A. LAND YOURSELF ON AN INDO BOAT TRIP AND YOU'LL SURF MORE THAN YOU EVER HAVE BEFORE. YOU'LL EXPERIENCE RASH, INCREDIBLE SUNBURN AND'LL REACH A LEVEL OF PERFORMANCE YOU'VE NEVER FOUND. TAJ ON A ROLL HERE, DOES HIS BEST TO BUTTER THE FLIP. B. THE POP SHUV-IT ON A PLAYFUL DAY IN THE WEST AUSTRALIAN DESERT. C. CAR CRASH PHOTOS ARE GRUESOME TOO. TINY ODDS HERE.

THE FUTURE

COMPLACENCY IS DEATH. THE MOMENT WE THINK WE'VE GOTTEN AS FAR AS WE CAN GO IS THE DAY WE DESERVE TO DIE.

Remember how a few years ago, hardly any airs were being made? Now there's guys throwing punts at every beach in the world. Well, here's the next stage: in five years, flips will be getting made as easily as an alley oop or air reverse. A flip will be normal. You wait.

FOR ALL YOU PUNTERS...

▶ Flips are the frontier, for now. I can't believe more crap like that does not get nailed already. And I'm not talking straps and jetskis, just your board, the wave and the double grab. I can appreciate all the crazy flips and rotations windsurfers like Rush Randall do but I'm not into the feeling of being locked in. It feels dangerous and, besides, we should be able to do it without them. I've been coming close but landing off the back. Parko's really good at them too, and I've seen Andy getting close in Hawaii. I've been trying to do full-rotation airs in my air reverses so I land back facing the beach rather than backwards and spinning around.

▶ Some days I paddle out and feel I can make any air I go for. That's the time to think about new stuff. When you've got that confidence and you're on that roll, you need to find your sections and nail your new move. I always forget about it, though. I just froth out, racing toward a section, do a normal punt with my normal grab and make it. Then I'm like, "Aah, I should have tried something new."

▶ I want to nail a frontside varial. That's when you do a frontside punt, throw your board around mid-air and land backwards. Seems like you could do it frontside or backside. I've made a few little Supermans and done some really high ones using the ski but it's just too scary to land when you're at that height. Fundamentally, they're pretty basic, even though they're only new. Double grabs are an easy air. A Superman is just a double grab with your legs kicked out. The challenge will be the variations in the air, say spinning your board around mid-air.

▶ I'm sure there are lots of rad air guys who do new tricks all the time. But new tricks only get noticed when someone in the limelight – like Parko, Mick or Bruce – nail them. Those air guys do crazy gear. If I had the amount of time they have to practise crap like they do, I could really nail something. I seriously wanna travel around surfing rippable waves, where every section is a ramp. That's all I wanna do. I just don't get enough chance to do it. You hurt yourself doing airs, too, and I can't afford to do that at this stage of my career.

▶ I like right pointbreaks with a light onshore making the waves a little bit crumbly. Light onshore or blowing toward you, like those classic, glassy conditions you get in Indo. Any kind of waves with a little ramp at the end or waves that run down the line. Think about all this next time you pull up at a break that's begging for punts. Get out there with the idea in your head that you're about to do something you've never done before. And don't think you can't invent a maneuver. There's still plenty left. I've got a couple in my head that I'm not ready to let out yet. But, for starters, who's done a 720, huh? A carving three-o into a 360 on the face. These moves are waiting for someone to do 'em. May as well be you...

TB TIP

SHARK ALERT. If you see a shark it doesn't mean it's hell bent on tearing you apart. Be cool, don't panic and catch the next wave in. Oh yeah, and try not to splash too much. I think it'd only be worth going in if it was a massive feeding frenzy. Easy.

SEQUENCE: RESPONDEK

CONTRIBUTORS

Twiggy: Kevin "Twiggy" Sharland is a close friend of TB's who just happens to be a damn good photographer. Currently travelling on the road with Taj and, when home, staying at his crib, Twigg has an access to the kid other photographers can only dream about. Is responsible for the outrageous photograph of Taj performing a Superman on page 004.

Sub-editors
Fred Pawle, Tim Macdonald, Derek Rielly, Sam McIntosh

Design
Emma Wicks, Campbell Milligan

Photographers
Anders, Bosko, Jack English, Joli, Tim Jones, Chris Van Lennep, Bill Morris, Jason Murray, Scott Needham, Tony Nolan, Derek Rielly, Rondog, Paul Sargeant, Nathan Smith, Stamos, Wheels.

THANKS: Brian Robbins, Hollywood, Ron Blakey, Timbo, Al Miles, BC, Bobbat Austin, Rod Dahlberg, Angie Daska, Pats Frost, Jeff Baldwin, John Malloy, Liam Fitzgerald, Circe Wallace, Mel Butler, Sam Hanson, Jack, Lindy, James, Tom, Suse, Vance and Nancy Burrow, Joel Patterson, Mike Perry, Ozzie Wright, Greg Scott, Tony Nolan, Matt George, Steve Zeldin, Vaughan Blakey, Marc Kozai, Nuords, Rictor, Stamos, Gezza Blake, Jean-Marc Parodi, Rog Sharp, Luke Jeffrey, Matt Gye, Rendog.

John Respondek: Only 25, yet already listed as a senior photographer in prestigious magazines, *Surfer* and *Waves*. A genuine natural talent, John's first photo shoot yielded four pages. Soon after, he was courted by Australia's biggest surfing magazines keen to secure exclusive rights to his images. John is a regular guest at Taj's crib and often travels with the kid, hence his thick file of TB images.

Fred Pawle: Fred Pawle developed his surfing in the lacklustre beachbreaks of Perth, Western Australia, and has spent most of his life since seeking classic solo sessions in the world's crappiest waves. Fred has written about surfing for every major Australian newspaper and surfing mag, as well as some American ones. Has worked on pornographic magazines twice in his distinguished career. Is currently writing a novel, *Splash*, a sharp-witted expose on newspaper life. Fred was responsible for most of the sub-editing in this book.

Derek Rielly: A raw and brilliant talent, Derek ruled the surf magazine world through the nineties with his magazine, *ASL*. Fond of controversy, Derek's humour and philosophy that the reader deserved honest reporting regularly steered the title into hot water (advertisers pulling out, law suits from disgruntled subjects, surfers threatening violence), though the readers frothed on it. Since leaving in 1999, Derek has launched the five-language Pan European title, *Surf Europe*, briefly edited Australia's biggest men's magazine, wrote a movie, a novel (*Sweet Light Crude*), is a partner in RollingYouth Press, and is co-creator of Stab magazine.

Scott Aichner: Fit, powerful, thinks about his photos and gets closer with his camera-rig than anyone. Lives on the North Shore. Has taken over the mantle of world's best wide-angle photographer from South African Chris Van Lennep. Scott is thirty years old. Has at least 10 left on the front line.

Bosko: A veteran of the surf photography game, Peter "Bosko" Boskovic has been shooting for close to two decades. Bosko lives in Newcastle and is a close friend of Luke Egan and Matt Hoy and it was his photos of these two surfing greats and, later, his sparkling work in the water that has made him such a bankable commodity.

Steve Sherman: A strong inspiration to all those surfers – the Malloys, Jack Johnson, Rob Machado, Conan Hayes and Kelly Slater – who've suddenly developed a passion for photography. Uses old Swedish equipment and mainly black-and-white film to create images that breathe and bleed on the page. Sherm shot the cover image of this book.

Greg Webber: Just the most creative shaper in the whole freakin' world. Taj Burrow's exclusive shaper. Also, a brilliant pop philosopher.

A. JOHN RESPONDEK, COMPLETE WITH PERSONALISED SHIRT, LAUNCHES OUT OF THE WATER AT THE PRECISE MOMENT HE SEES TAJ ABOUT TO PUNT. THIS IS ONE OF THE REASONS WHY HE IS A PHOTOGRAPHY GREAT IN THE MAKING.

portait by rielly

Greg Webber carves the blades Taj Burrow rides.

The hottest surfers on the tour pay cash for his designs.

Email him. He gets off on taking ordinary surfers to higher places.

TB GEAR

IF YOU LIKED THIS BOOK, YOU MIGHT BE TEMPTED TO DROP COIN ON THE FOLLOWING ITEMS...

SHOE

TB2B by Globe

Here's a tricky shoe. Solid enough to whack around on your skateboard, slick enough to please the authorities at school, and if you're a little older, will get you into any crook nightclub joint you want to get creepy at. These Globes are made out of synthetic nubuck (a leather-like material, no innocent bovine is slaughtered for the skin) and they come in six colors. I'm a size nine and favor the metal/black combo.

SANDAL

The Taj Slide

Fur on the front, rubber underneath. A recipe for comfort and style. Is there a more sublime feeling than the wind rushing through your hooves? A step above rubber slippers, you can dance, enter bars, impress the chicklets, impress the world.

DECK GRIP

Taj Grip by Creatures of Leisure

If you're going to punt, get this under your back hoof. The raised arch bar gives you something to push off, the tailpad lets you know you're standing in the right spot, and the rubber protects your tail — so thin it's the most vulnerable part of your board.

MOVIES

Sabotaj

My old boy Vance plus Rictor and Jack McCoy put together my first profile video. There's a lot of gear from around Yallingup and Margs, stuff from the French beachies and even a bit of dirt gets talked about with a couple of continental ladies. As an aside, I landed a floater on the jetski Jack McCoy was filming from. Pays not to get close to a frothing kid.

Montaj

It won the *Surfer* mag poll's Video of the Year, 2002, so it must have hit a few nails. Again, like Sabotaj, it's full of West Oz gear plus the requisite Mentawais trip and France, Gold Coast, Portugal, all those ports the tour calls into, sirens raging. I spent two weeks with Matt Gye editing this, all day and all night. Torture.

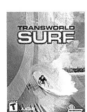

VIDEO GAME

Transworld Surf

I froth over this game, and just 'cause my rank little head's in there. You can surf Kirra, Tavarua, Huntington, Pipe, Hossegor, G-Land. You can pretend you're Shane Dorian, Andy Irons, Tim Curran, among others. Reef girls on jetskis take you back out to the lineup. Hang about too long under water and you'll be devoured by sharks. One of the coolest things is if you're learning to backside tuberide, this thing is so real, you get a virtual tour of, say, Andy or Doz styling in the tube. I went into the studio for a series of shots and, when the game came out, I was amazed at how realistic my character's cutbacks were to mine.

SURFING'S A STRANGE GAME. IT'S DIFFICULT TO LEARN AND JUST COMMUNICATING WITH THE COOL KIDS WHO HAVE ALL THE ANSWERS CAN SEEM IMPOSSIBLE. BELOW IS A SPECIAL SURFING DICTIONARY TO HELP YOU INTERPRET WHAT YOU HEAR IN THE LINEUP AND ON THE BEACH... SOME I USE, OTHERS I WOULDN'T LET NEAR MY TONSILS.

a-frame. When a wave breaks left and right simultaneously. (See also: peak.)

aggro. Aggression in the water. It happens everywhere, look for the signs and steer clear of it.

aerial. Any maneuver where the surfer and board leave the wave and hit the air-waves is broadly classed as an aerial, though there are stacks of variations. Pioneers of these spectacular moves include Davey Smith (USA), Christian Fletcher (USA) and Martin Potter (South Africa).

air. (See: aerial)

alley oop. An aerial variation invented and named by Californian Tim Curran. The alley-oop is a forehand aerial 180 where the rotation is backside (tail first) rather than frontside (that is, a natural footer spins in a clockwise direction. Unlike a standard frontside 360, which goes anti-clockwise). Confused? Watch *Montaj*, see if you can pick 'em up.

arch bar. The raised section of a tailpad. It's there to help you find the centre of your board and to give you a lever when you want to launch a chop-hop or an air or whatever.

bail. A parachuting term now used by surfers to describe any situation where an inglorious sudden escape is the best option, such as throwing your board away as a set approaches.

awesome. Literally, full of awe. Awesome is used by surfers of stunted vocabularies to describe anything from good three-foot beachbreaks to wild 20-foot Waimea. Like anything, if you overuse it the word loses its power.

backhand. Riding with your back to the wave. Interestingly, some surfers never quite get the hang of backhand surfing despite it opening up at least half the world's waves. Don't neglect your backhand.

backside. Generally means the same as backhand though it can be used by technical air kids to describe the direction of their rotation.

barb. Your penis. (see: prong, champignon.)

barrel. The green room, the womb, the part of the wave that is enclosed by the throwing lip and which you can stand inside once you develop the sort of steely nerve necessary to place yourself in such a precarious position.

beachbreak. Waves that break on sand, not rock. Apart from Mexico's Puerto Escondido, beachbreaks are a tame affair compared to reefs. Great place to punt and get loose.

beak. Your nose. (See also: buges and bugle.)

bearded. Excited. Frothing so much it appears you are wearing a beard of foam.

birdman. To kick out of a wave and fly into the air, usually just before closeouts.

bitchen. American word from the sixties that means really, really good. Tragic or cool? I veer toward the former. Use it at your peril.

blank. The foam in the middle of a board. Sculpted by shapers, encased by glassers.

boardshorts, boardies. The nylon shorts you wear to protect and shield your prong. Stylewise, avoid elastic waists, make sure they are long enough to pass over the knee and don't fear wearing white. The velcro will hide your prong.

bodyboard. A small soft craft designed for riding waves on your stomach. Don't laugh but if you don't have the time or the persistence to stick this surfing game out, this isn't such a bad option. You can experience the thrill of riding a wave quicker and more safely than on a fiberglass board.

bomb. An especially good wave. Usually the biggest set of the day.

bonzer. Type of bottom curve where the forward concave leads into a double concave popularized by the Campbell brothers in the seventies.

boost. To launch an air. To boost is to impress.

bottom turn. The most precious turn you'll learn in surfing. Without it, you've got a one-way ticket to the shore.

bugle. Nose. On your face, or on your board.

bumbat. I guess the bumbat became famous in the video, *Sabotaj*. My mate Rictor made it up. Loosely, it's a board with a round nose and wide tail. Whenever I surf in contests in the United States, the commentators always say things like, "Yeah, see him riding that wombat in *Sabotaj*. How is that thing?" It's so annoying. It's a bumbat, you gibbons, not a wombat.

button mushroom. Your prong after two-hour surf in boardies in winter.

caned. Worked, smoked, kicked, toasted etc.

champy. Short for champignon, a delicate button mushroom used in cooking. Used to describe the above condition, eg. "The surf was *so* cold, I'm going to be sporting a miserable champy all day long."

cheese whiz. Using the chop of a wave to launch an on-the-face air. (See also: chop hop).

chinese wax job. Getting wax on the bottom of your board from having the deck of another board placed on it. An evil, all-too-common occurrence.

chop hop. The first brick in the golden road to proper airs (see page 122).

choppy. Surf that is being blown about by a strong, gusty wind, usually onshore.

cans. Breasts, usually larger than average. Below average, titlets.

cave. A good-size tube. No crouch, no bent legs.

claim. To put your hands in the air, hoot, wipe your nose, look to the beach that shows you're bearded with what you've just done. Do it with caution but if you're stoked, let it out, I reckon.

clean. Smooth conditions. The older you get, the more pedantic you get with hunting clean conditions.

clubbies. Surf lifesavers. Once the sworn enemy of surfers in Australia. We understand each other a bit better these days.

coin. Money. Cash. The green.

concave. A groovy but subtle scoop running down the bottom of a surfboard. Gives the board lift. This translates into a kinda weightless speed especially noticeable on takeoff.

corner. The green face. The unbroken part of the wave where you can light up.

cowabunga. Today, way more *Teenage Mutant Ninja Turtles* than surf, an old school term meant to express exhilaration.

credit card airs. Tiny airs. Airs so small you could lay flat only a credit card between the bottom of the board and the wave's face.

creepy. Tuning chicks with an eye to some sort of freaky sexual activity.

crook. No good. Rankshank. If something's crook it stinks.

curl. The lip of a wave.

cutback. When you're out there on the face, miles away from the pocket, and you turn your board around and head back to the source.

craft. Surfboard.

cloth. Soft fiberglass matting used by glassers, and by you when fixing dings.

casio. Casino. MGM Grand, Flamingos, New York New York, Caesar's Palace etc. Fortunes won and lost on every deal. Open 24 hours and the drinks and ladies are free (almost).

caught inside. Stranded in the impact zone with a set about to break. In small to medium surf, this will test your duckdiving skills. In big surf, it will test your courage and strength. The hardest part? Going under waves instead of riding them.

closeout. A wave that breaks along its entire length at the same time. (see also: closet.)

closet. Cool speak for above.

corduroy. Swell that is strong and well organized, marching so uniformly toward the coast that it looks like corduroy. What a sight to behold!

crazy. Very good. Ridiculously overused by me.

crib. House. Living quarters.

delamination. Separation of glass from a board's blank. Better known as an air bubble.

deck. The top of a surfboard.

ding. Holes and shatters and breaks in your board. No upside to these little things. The result of being run over, clumsy or getting close and personal with the rocks.

dirty turd. Spend time around surfers in the WCT and you'll hear this one on high rotation. Last place in a WCT event is 33rd. Get it?

don the apron. To really make a meal of something. To butcher it. To put on the blue-and-white butcher's apron.

double-up. A swell that has been joined by the one behind to create a thick, heaving two-for-the-price-of-one wave.

down the line. (1) A fast-breaking, longish sort of wave, such as "Kirra's a real down-the-line wave". (2) The section ahead, such as, "I was looking down the line, trying to find a section to waft."

downstairs. Genitalia. Loins. Little dicky or puss-puss.

downtown. (See: downstairs.)

dropped wallet. A turn invented by Tom Curren and popularized by Margo in the early nineties. It describes the motion of your board running wild mid-turn and you keep a hold of it with your front foot and by laying back in the wash. While in the wash, you get your back foot on the board and exit from the wash standing. Term invented by hot New Zealand surfer, Maz Quinn.

duckdive. To submerge your board while paddling so an oncoming wave can pass overhead. An important move. Without it, you will never learn, because you will spend all your time merely trying to get to the lineup.

dumped. To cop a two-footer on the head and a bit of sand in the tweeds. More likely to be used by those who don't often go to the beach.

egg. As in the drug, ecstasy. Steer clear of these things unless you want to move to the inner city, get real skinny, turn pasty white and be hardly recognizable to your mates in a few months time. And that's just what it does to the outside.

face. The green, unbroken part of the wave. Where you can lay down all the hot moves you've learnt from this book.

fading. Dropping down the face and drifting back towards the whitewater. Usually done to get you back into the pocket, but is also useful if you've dropped in on one of your mates, and want him to eat wash while you flare. Warning: don't do this to locals, especially in Hawaii.

fair bits. A cooler version of saying "Yeah right" when a friend winds up the hyperbole machine, eg. When your mate tells you he had sex with four girls in one night, you could reply with a flat tire followed by, "fair bits."

fat. Slow moving, chubby waves, with no pocket. Difficult to do your freaky moves on for lack of steepness on the face.

fin throw. A maneuver, closely related to the waft, whereupon the fins are thrown out in one spectacular motion; a move usually done to benefit friends watching from behind.

fin waft. A split-second from an air, a supercharged re-entry where the fins appear briefly above the lip.

figgity. Fifty. Used when talking coin, eg, "Lost figgity skins at the casio."

fit. Good, real good. Eg, "The luts round here are lookin' fit."

figs. Balls. Testicles.

fin. Usually in groups of three, attached to the bottom of a board near the tail. Responsible for drive and stability. (Want a challenge? If you've got removable fins, take 'em out and try surfing a finless board. Hint: use your rail to hold you in the face.)

flare. To light it up. To hit exceptional form.

flat tire. When you want to cut someone down, you let out a sharp spittle of air through pursed lips, like the sound of air leaving a tire. eg. A mate incorrectly states: "Waves were six foot today" to which you reply: "Pfffffffffft."

flats. Out in front of a breaking wave. Do a big psycho punt and launch too far forward and you'll be in the flats. Really tough to make airs and floaters in this part of town but easy to toast your knee and ankle joints.

flip. A 360 air. As this book goes to print, nobody has ever made a flip and landed back on the wave. We're still landing on the back of the wave. In five years, I reckon flips will be as common as airs are today.

floater. Riding across the top of the lip. Popularized by Australian surfer Mark Sainsbury in the eighties and used to great effect by Luke Egan this century.

foam. The broken part of the wave. The white gear that'll mow you down and cause you a fountain of grief.

forehand. See frontside.

freight train. A wave that grinds along fast and relentlessly.

frontside. A wave you can ride with your face and chest facing the wave (a right if you're a naturalfooter, a left if you ride goofy). Also, in skateboarding talk, a move where you spin clockwise (naturalfooters).

frothing. As in foaming at the mouth. Terribly excited, so excited in fact you might even lose some salmon.

full suit. Long-armed steamer. Covers you from ankles to wrists.

gee. Grand. One thousand dollars. Chump change if you're a pro surfer; a lot if you're still at school.

geese. A fool, a bad person, an oxygen thief.

gibbon. By definition, a type of monkey. In our case, a dork.

gibboin. As above, customized and mutated. Both insults work equally well.

gnarly. Heavy, though this heaviness is relative. A moody chick can be gnarly. So can 40-foot Jaws.

golden tonsils. An exceptional storyteller/comedian/public speaker.

gone bad. When a mate turns on you, eg. "Wheels has gone bad."

goofy. Strange cats who ride with their right foot forward, eg. Tom Carroll, Luke Egan, Occ etc.

goofyfooter. The full-length version of goofy.

grill. To smoke marijuana.

griller. Someone who smokes weed. A crazy griller will almost always be paranoid and prone to snapping.

grilled. Someone who is affected from smoking weed.

grillover. The resulting comedown of being grilled: dry mouth, slowed brain, depression, evil breath.

grom. Broadly, a surfer younger than 17 and without a driver's license. Short blokes can milk the grom tag well into their late teens. (See also, grommet.)

grom abuse. Physical or mental abuse directed at a grom. Kinda weird and almost always involving turds, asses and young men being tied up.

grommet. The envy of every surfer alive. Young, irresponsible and usually the best surfer at the beach. (see: grom.)

groundswell. Waves that have moved well away from the area where they were generated, and are lined up. Swells like these aren't so great for beachies with crap banks but are dream swells for points and reefs. (See also, corduroy.)

gutter. Deep water where waves don't break. Also a favored hang for sharkies.

gun. Nothing to do with bullets or semi-automatics. The most accepted term for a big-wave board.

hack. A jagged direction change, eg., "Check out Sunny's mad hack." Also, a surf, eg., "Want to go for a quick hack down back beach?"

hardener. The chemical catalyst used with resin to make it go, uh, hard.

head dip. When you lean your head forward closer to the wave because it feels like you're in the tube. Likely reality? Your ass is sticking out and your head is in the foam.

heapa. As in heap of crap. Not good. Ordinary.

heavy. When you appoint a level of danger or seriousness to something. Could be a fatal chick, a wave at Pipe or a call you made on a buddy that was a little too far.

hell. Good. Sick. This term is not so popular these days, but is still effective.

Hobbities. Hobgood brothers, CJ and Damien. Both goofyfooters with real similar styles. Ceej was the world champ in 2001.

hole. Tube. Usually a big one.

hoof. Your foot. Your feet are hooves. Driving the hoof through the tail of your board isn't cool.

Ice. Nathan Webster's nickname for his Audi stolen from snowboarder talk. Cloth seats, no turbo, pretty standoid vehicle.

ice-cream headaches. The feeling your head gets when you duckdive in very cold water. You think your head is going to explode. Why? Extremes of hot and cold on the face turn the brainstem on so much it freaks out the things called dura cells, thus producing pain in the head.

impact zone. Where the waves break. You can tell this by all the furious foam action.

inside. (1) Tubed. (2) Surfer closest to the breaking part of the wave.

jack. When a wave grows very quickly and appears to stands up. Difficult to catch.

kick out. To exit a wave with style, like an aggressive jam on the tail. If you make a tube, use the speed to lay down a nice hack, don't just kick out. You'll be glad you did when those flat days come around.

killer. Exceptionally good.

kitesurfing. Real popular in the past few years with guys who have made the jump from sailboards (windsurfers). Involves a double-ended board (often a wakeboard), a sail and a good length of rope. The biggest rattle about 'em though is when you're groveling out in two-foot surf and there's guys out there doing 20-foot airs.

kook. Relax, beginners. If you're cool in the water, you're not a kook, not in my book anyway. Kooks are aggressive, egotists who surf with a rank style. Kooks can also refer to any gent or lady who behaves in a generally crook manner.

layback. Old-school backside move. Mid-turn, you throw your body back into the face. A popular way to ride backside barrels in the seventies.

leash. American for a legrope.

left. (see: lefthander.)

lefthander. A wave which breaks from left to right as viewed from the beach. Frontside to a goofyfooter.

leggie. Legrope. The item which attaches your surfboard to your leg.

legrope. Two schools of thought here. First, not only are they a necessity when surfing near rocks or in crowds, where a loose board could wind up badly dinged or nailing a gibbon, but they encourage bad surfing by not forcing you to make the move. On the other hand, surfing without them feels free and easy, and when you do wipeout, the swim to the beach is good fitness training. I'm with the former. If you're not falling, you're not improving. By the time you've swum to get a board you've probably missed one or two waves. You're there to surf. Your mate with the leash is getting better than you at three times the speed.

licked. The result of a wipeout or a fight. eg. "I got licked on that wave."

light it up. To hit form. Two psycho turns in a row is enough to have your mates saying, "Whoa, the fool's lighting it up!"

lineup. Where the waves are. The impact zone is where they break, the lineup is where you sit and wait for the things.

lip. The part of the wave that folds, breaks and smashes. You can hit it, dive under it, sit beneath it or get your leg broken by it. Depends on the wave.

lobster. An Australian 20-dollar note.

long john. A freaky rubber suit that's long in the legs and a singlet up top. Hilarious looking thing but, to be fair, they do make even the weepsiest rig look spectacular.

long-sleeve spring. Short-leg, long-arm wetsuit.

lull. A break between waves. A good time to jump off the rocks. Jump! Go, dammit! Jump!

luts. Sexually aggressive young ladies.

Mace. My nickname for my sweaty black Audi. All leather, kitted up and complete with techtronic gear.

Momentum generation. A pack of clean-livin' kids who emerged from the US in the early nineties in a series of videos titled, *Momentum*. Their style of surfing was new, electric and what frothing groms the world over were looking for. Produced by Taylor Steele, the vids were a new formula too: short, fast action-packed and the polar opposite to slower, more spiritual surf movies being pumped out by the surf companies. And the stars? You know who they are: Kelly Slater, Shane Dorian, Kalani Robb, Rob Machado and Tim Curran.

natural. (see: naturalfooter.)

naturalfooter. Surfing with your left foot forward. (see: regular footer)

necked. Drunk.

North Shore. Though many cities around the world pack an area called the North Shore, in surfing it's the North Shore of Oahu in Hawaii. A short stretch that houses Waimea, Sunset, Pipeline, Rocky Point and a host of other evil waves that are dying to test the capacity of your lungs.

nosedive. When, unintentionally, your surfboard penetrates the water nose first. Usually happens on steep, sudden take-offs. (see: pearling.)

noseriding. Standing on the beak of a longboard.

Nuad. Nathan Webster. Good friend who drives an Audi similar to mine. He called his car the Ice. I've named mine the Mace. The Ice has no crazy tech gear, no kit and cloth seats. The Ice is similar in appearance to the Mace from the outside. However, the Mace is a far more superior vehicle.

Occy. (1) Elastic strap for tying boards to roof racks. (2) Some bloke from Cronulla, Sydney. Won a title or something.

off it. Same as over it. You can be off a mate with an attitude or off going to work or school because the waves are pumping.

offshore. Wind blowing from land to ocean. The best wind for creating tubes.

onion. Dings that look like onion rings.

onshore. Wind blowing from ocean to land. The best wind for airs.

oop. Pronounced ewwp. Cool speak for an alley oop.

out the back. Beyond where the average-size waves are breaking, eg. "Check that bomb out the back!"

over it. Had enough, not interested. If you've been surfing perfect Kirra but have only caught one crappy wave in three hours, there's a good chance you'd be over it.

over the falls. Falling with the lip of the wave because you either blew the take-off or tried to paddle up the face and didn't quite make it. Looks ridiculous. If you've got a chick watching from the shore, her opinion of you will be seriously diminished. Usually not dangerous, though. You get pushed straight under the wave and come back up pretty quickly.

paddle. To surf, eg. "Going for a paddle. Keen?"

pad. Place with a roof and bed. Could be an apartment or a house.

parachute. Large T-shirts popular with surf companies. Always go at least one size smaller when buying tees, eg. If you're typically a medium kid, go small.

pegs. Teeth. Hint: Use a straw when drinking sugar-rich beverages like fruit juice or the fizzy gear. The gear'll only hit the back pegs on the way down, saving your pearly front ones from turning brown and decaying.

park it. To stall and get tubed by dragging your kicker in the water. Used mostly for backside tuberiding.

peak. A wave that breaks left and right. (See also: a-frame.)

pearling. To nose dive. Paddle hard, get down the face and keep your weight on your back foot and you'll avoid pearling.

pigdog. The most common backside tuberiding style. Hunch over your board and grab your outside rail with your trailing hand. The stance is low and sturdy, like a dog.

pill. Ecstasy, pinger. See egg. Evil things.

pin. A small prong.

pintail. Narrow tail. Good for guns.

pinger. Ecstasy. See egg.

pins. Skinny legs, usually mine.

plan shape. The outline of your surfboard. If your board's plan shape is wider through the tail, your board will perform better in small waves.

pop shuv-it. Tech move that is like a chop hop but your board spins 180 degrees under your feet. Make one and you'll finish the move in a stance opposite to the one you own. If you're natural, you'll ride out goofy.

pound. To make love in a hard and aggressive manner. To pound at your lover's pavement without respite.

prone. To ride on your stomach. You could be paddling for a wave, the wash knocks you down and you miss the best part of the wave because you were riding prone.

prone out. To go from standing to laying on your stomach. If you've just nailed a hot closeout reo, the prone ride to the sand is a glory trail.

prong. Penis. (see also: barb.)

psycho. Really good. Crazy (told you I use it a lot).

punt. To launch an air.

pumped. Psyched.

putting on the beard. A male partaking in oral sex with a female. Better than you think, exercises the jaw and opens up an Alladin's Cave of sexual delights.

Q-cell. The white powdery gear you mix with resin to fill holes in your board. It's lighter than resin and it's easier to sand.

quiver. Your boards. Two boards is a quiver, 10 boards is a quiver. One board is one board.

rad. Short for radical. Old-school but still kinda cool 'cause it rolls off the tongue so easily.

rank. No good. Crook.

rank lips. Mutation of above.

rankshank. Further mutation.

rattled. Emotionally shaken. You might get rattled when a good-lookin' man comes into a bar and your chick is visibly impressed or, more likely, you'll be rattled on your first trip to Hawaii and you see a 10-foot set cap out the back and know that you have about five seconds before you get absolutely licked.

redback. Australian 20-dollar note. Like a lobster, it's red.

re-entry. To hit the lip in the pocket with the aim of gaining speed.

regular. An American naturalfooter.

reo. (see: re-entry.)

reverse. Invented by Kelly Slater. Literally, to go backwards, though if someone tells you they just did a reverse it means they did a reo and kept spinning through 360 degrees.

rhino chaser. (see: gun.)

Rictor. My filmer Rick Jakovich and the man responsible for all the cool 16mm shots in my vids. Tricky cat, one of my best mates. He doesn't say much but what he does is pure platinum. Invents words at such a furious rate you could fill this entire glossary with meanings.

ride. Car, eg. "Dave's new Ford truck is a sweet ride. Even sweeter when he goes out of his way to pick me up for a hack."

rig. A torso, usually a good one. Either male or female.

right. (see: righthander.)

righthander. When you're looking from the beach, a wave that breaks from right to left.

round. Waves that feature a barrel so big it isn't almond shaped but... round. Teahupoo is round, Huntington isn't. (See also: square.)

round tail. Uh, exactly that: a round tail. Used by ultra-smooth Californian Rob Machado.

salmon. Pronouncing the word "semen" phonetically.

set. A group of waves. Waves always come in sets, except in a gutless wind swell.

seuss. To improve. To seuss an old board is to clean it up. Pronounced with a "z". (see page 060)

shack. Barrel. Tube.

shaka. Hand movement created when thumb and pinkie finger are left straight and three middle fingers tuck into your palm, accentuated more with a quick wrist twisting. Expression of joy. Real popular in Hawaii and Tahiti. Double shaka involves the same process but with two hands. If you're in a throaty cave approaching a photog, it's not a real cool way to get your photo in the mag. Keep it cool in there.

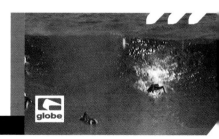

shockwave. When you ride a tube and the inside off the wave kicks back under your feet. Usually when you're deep in the tube.

shooter. Surfboard.

short-arm steamer. Long leg, short-arm wetsuit.

shortie. (1) Short board. The one you use most often, in waves up to, say, six feet. (2) A short-john wetsuit. Short legs, singlet top. Very kooky.

short john. A one-piece rubber swimsuit for men. Teak. (See also, long john.)

shoulder. The part of the face where the wave hasn't broken. Surf good Pipeline and chances are you'll spend your time on the shoulder frozen by the crowd and the sheer power of the place.

shuv-it. When you do an air and spin your board under your feet so you land on it backwards. The momentum will spin the board around and you'll be riding opposite to your stance. If you're goofy, you'll do a shove-it and be riding natural. (see also: pop shuv-it.)

sick. Really good.

sickhunt. We live in a world of moral hypocrisy: we got bombs, wars, all sorts of gnarly gear and yet the media and everyone freaks out at certain arrangements of letters. Crazy, eh? So what's wrong with a word to describe the outrageous, creepy, cool behavior of men at their finest? Nothing, kids. Words don't cause no harm. A sickhunt is someone like my good friend Damon Nicholls who lives his life as if there's only one week left in it.

sick prong. An expression of delight, eg. "That surf was *so* sick prong."

single fin. One fin, one line. Not too common but great to ride to smooth out your surfing and make you turn using your rails.

sink it. To make love.

sinking it. Currently making love.

ski. Jetski. As in PWC. As in personal watercraft. As in Wave Runner. As in the funnest thing in the world.

skins. Dollars. Cash.

slash. A turn on the face, usually with plenty of spray.

slay. The act of surfing. You see a mate at night and he asks, "You slay?" If the waves were good that day, you will probably reply, "Hell yeah."

smoked. To wipe out. (see also: licked.)

smoker. A good ride. Also, a male receiving oral sex.

Snake. Jake Paterson. The man I grew up surfing with. Pipe Master. Co-owner of my jetski.

squash. A type of tail shape.

spit. When a wave tubes for long enough, it coughs out a mist. As a surfer this is the greatest thing you'll ever experience because it usually means you've successfully negotiated a tube.

springie. (see: springsuit)

springsuit. Short-leg, short-arm wetsuit.

square. An extremely heavy, ledging barrel that forms the shape of a square when it breaks, eg., Shark Island, in Sydney.

stab. To punt.

stall. To slow down and wait for the wave to catch up to you. Most useful when sniffing the tube.

Stamos. Damon Nicholls. One of my best friends. One of the finest men on this Earth.

standoid. Mutation of standard.

steps. Buckles on the face of a wave breaking over shallow reef. Wild things, tough to get over. Only for experienced surfers. Shark Island in Sydney, Mavericks in California.

stinking it up. Making a terrible meal of a situation whether it's a wave or picking up girls, whatever.

stoked. Happy, bearded.

stoned. High on the wacky weed, marijuana. (see also: grilled.)

stoner. (see: griller.)

straighthander. A wave that breaks neither left nor right. A filthy closeout. No good to anyone, except if you're practicing drops, bottom turns and chop hops if there's a little bacckwash.

struck. The combination of a pain in your gut and a rock in your bowel. A polite way to say you need to take a crap.

styling. Ruling, killing it.

steamer. Long arm, long-legged wetsuit. Full suit.

stringy DNA. Cool word for semen, eg. "I haven't rained my stringy DNA for almost a week." The term has mutated into "genetic code". Brought into this world by Mr Derek Rielly, surf journalist.

stupid. Impressive or evil. A stupid wave is most likely a thick, heaving bone-breaker. A stupid turn is most likely some bizarre unmakeable fin throw that is somehow made.

sucky. Punchy, hollow waves.

suit. Cool speak for wetsuit.

suit up. To wrap yourself in neoprene. To put on a wetsuit.

sunk it. Post love. Salmon rained.

surf mat. Old school blow-up mat ridden on your stomach. Also called surfoplane.

surf nazi. A Californian term for a surfer who lives and breathes surfing.

superman. Dirt-bike maneuver, now done by surfers. A double-grab air where you kick your legs out, hold board above your head and drop it back under your feet before you land. The first Superman wasn't made until this century.

swallow tail. A "W" tail shape named after the tail of the bird, the swallow.

sweaty. Good times, not perspiration. A sweaty tube is a nice little shack.

sweet. Cool. No dramas. If you go over the falls on a six-footer and come up unscathed, you're sweet.

sweet spot. The spot on your board where your feet feel, well, sweet. Every turn you go for, your placement feels perfect. Some people reckon it's when your back foot is positioned directly above your fins but I think this is far too general an assumption.

tail. The back 12" of your surfboard.

tailpad. Adhesive grip, stuck deckside on the tail of your surfboard.

tank. Big board. Could be a mal, could be something that big kids Sunny Garcia or Luke Egan ride.

tarp up. To sport a condom. Sheath that prong and rut safe.

teak. Crap (which is the same color as teak). Like getting struck, it's a family-friendly way of voicing your dislike of something.

The Rock. Oahu, especially the North Shore.

titlets. Titties that are too small to be called tits but with enough curve and lift to be impressive. Another Derek Rielly invention.

three-o. 360.

thruster. The most common fin configuration. Invented by Narrabeen surfer/shaper Simon Anderson in 1980. Melded the advantages of single fins and twin fins into one three-finned surfboard. It's testimony to the durability of the design that more than 20 years later, everyone still rides thrusters.

trim. The way you move across the face of a wave. Any surfer who can trim well and go fast is a great surfer.

trough. The kicker. Your asshole. Also, the sucking section off the back of a wave once it breaks. When floating you've got to get off the lip before you fall in the trough.

trunks. Boardies.

tube. Stand inside one and your life will change forever. (see also: barrel.)

tweaked. (1) Stoned, grilled. (2) Damaged, eg. A tweaked knee will leave you out of the water for weeks. (3) A slight but significant movement, eg. Tweak your ankles while dropping down the face to fade.

tweeds. Underwear. Bikini style bathing trunks or lil man panties.

twigs. Skinny legs.

twin fin. Board with two fins. Made famous by four-time world champ Mark Richards from Newcastle, Australia. Overshadowed by the more user-friendly three-finned thruster, though still the craft of choice for some good surfers in small waves.

upstairs. Your headspace. Brain.

varial. Any shove-it where you spin the board with your hand.

vest. A rubber singlet.

waft. (see: fin waft.)

wash. Whitewater.

wax. That beautiful gear you coat your board with every session. At around a buck, it will make the difference between a good and bad session.

wax comb. A stiff plastic comb with sharp claws that you use to rough up your slippery wax job to create at least some sorta grip. Use only if fresh wax is in short supply.

white caps. When the ocean has so much wind on it that it's causing small lips to crumble miles out to sea. Common with onshore winds though possible in an offshore.

wedge. (1) A swell that has bounced off a breakwall or headland, concentrating its power. A wedging three-foot wave can have the power of a six-footer. (2) Any sucky wave. (3) A fried slice of potato.

weed. (1) Marijuana. (2) Skinny kid. (3) Cool speak for seaweed.

weeping eye. What your prong has after it's picked up a disease.

weeps. Diseased, eg. "The wind went onshore. It was weeps."

wetsuit. Rubber outfit that keeps you warm by trapping a layer of water between you and the rubber and heating it up.

wettie. (see: wetsuit.)

windswell. Windwaves produced by local prevailing swell. Usually lumpy, messy swells. Good for throwing the fins, and punts into the wind.

windsurfing. Surfing with a sail. Who needs one?

wipeout. To crash while surfing.

wettie warmer. Urinating in your suit in the water.

wheels. Figs. Testicles.

yeouch. An expression of disappointment. Could be when your girl spazzes out at you for going surfing, or if a mate suddenly turns and goes bad.

FLICK BOOK STARTS HERE